STANDING IN THE GAP

By Jonathon Lewis

BALBOA.
PRESS

A DIVISION OF HAY HOUSE

Editing By: Michele Meres

Balboa Press books may be ordered through booksellers or by contacting:

Balboa Press
A Division of Hay House
1663 Liberty Drive
Bloomington, IN 47403
www.balboapress.com
1-(877) 407-4847

ISBN: 978-1-4525-4941-5 (e)
ISBN: 978-1-4525-4942-2 (sc)
ISBN: 978-1-4525-4940-8 (hc)

Library of Congress Control Number: 2012905195

Printed in the United States of America

Balboa Press rev. date: 04/18/2012

I would like to dedicate this book to the
two most influential people in my life.
My son Travis and my daughter Ashley.
Having the privilege of being their
father has been the grandest
pleasure in my life.
If it were not for them, this cndeavor
would not have been possible.

Preface

Ezekiel 22:30 (KJV)

_"I looked for a man among them who would build up the
wall and stand before me in the gap
on behalf of the land so I would not have to destroy it,
but I found none."_

Ezekiel was a prophet in the Kingdom of Israel who lived around 590 B.C. He grew up in Jerusalem and served as a priest in the Jewish Temple. He was among the second group exiled to Babylon, where he becomes a Prophet of God. In this book of the Old Testament, Ezekiel tries to warn the people of Jerusalem and the surrounding nations of Judah, that God has seen their corrupt ways and this is the reason for their exile. He sees the destruction of his beloved nation and has a conversation with God to dissuade him from destroying the land and rendering it totally and completely desolate, forever.

Ezekiel means "strengthened by God," and as God imparts to him these visions, Ezekiel tries to strengthen his people in captivity. He tries to "stand in the gap" created by their unrepentant ways. He sees the gap in the hedge of their protection, which led to the exile. He tries to understand God's mercy and compassion while also reconciling God's punishment for turning away from Him. Ezekiel also has visions of restoration and a re-gathering of the Israelites, to the point of rebuilding their temple to God in praise of His rescue. God's reconciliation to His people is a perfect example of how God can accept and love that which He creates, even when His order is not followed. Our returned—love for Him must cover our transgressions, through Christ Jesus.

In my life, there have been many circumstances that were reconciled or "covered" by someone standing in the gap. A gap created by sibling abuse, emotional and verbal distress, sexual molestation, and many poor decisions. My sexuality is reconciled to God because, simply put, I love Him and His Grace covers the rest. He has provided for me in so many undeniable ways, as I must not and cannot deny Him. I believe for many gay, lesbian, bisexual, and trans-gendered, that we have been deceived by people in authority and judged under the precept of God to such a damaging degree, that we have turned from God's love and deny Him the privilege of knowing us. We have been hurt in such a deep and profound way, we blame God for not accepting us. It is "people" who don't accept us, not God.

Today's "church" has drastically fallen away from Christian ideals and principles. They no longer seem to care about a person's soul, rather a rigid structure that only endorses an acceptable facsimile of themselves. This is certainly reflected in the discrimination displayed by many churches that seem to promote encouragement of their members to hide their prejudices behind their professed faith. Justifying their bigotry as "biblical" or "moral," when the facts implore many examples of adultery, sexual immorality, false witnessing and coveting exposed under close personal scrutiny. The church needs to clean up their act if they're going to continue vilifying the gay community. I have experienced many forms of discrimination for being gay and having Aids, all of which were hypocritical. God has never once judged me for being who I am, only for my actions. This is the same for gays and heterosexuals. God does not discriminate. Period.

My prayer for you, is that you absorb this information with a pure and compassionate heart. I believe it will help you understand "that" someone in your life who is touched by homosexuality and/or Aids. I hope this book will "Stand in the Gap" for you and help you search your heart for truth.

Contents

Chapter 1

Walls! What Walls?

You are my hiding place;
you will protect me from trouble;
and surround me with songs of deliverance.

Psalm 32:7 (NIV)

Struggling, struggling to break free. The pain was intense and I felt bound at every turn. My brother Jett had me in a half nelson. He was much larger than me, and it was nearly impossible to twist free from his snare. He liked to inflict pain, especially if he knew he was accomplishing his goal—to cause me as much pain as possible. His strong arm was around me from behind with a tight grip around my wrist, pinning my arm behind my back, with his other arm under my chin. His muscles were fully flexed and taut to prevent me from even a slight movement. Then something happened causing him to instantly release his grip, and I was able to break free. I turned to face him. I lunged with a hard left, my only jab. Pain! Pain! Pain! A concrete and plaster wall had stopped my force. The noise and the sudden jolt of my body woke my new bride sleeping next to me.

"Are you all right?" she asked. "What did you do?"

She clamored to turn on the light. I quickly grasped my hand, hoping it would ease the pain. I realized what I had done. The pain throbbed through every cell of my flesh. I just knew I had broken something. My thoughts for a quick second turned to my career. I was a draftsman and depended upon my right hand for a living. *Oh God! What had I done?* I thought. My wife went to the kitchen to fix me a bag of ice, I lay in pain thinking of the nightmare that had preceded. I felt deep in my soul that the abuse from Jett was not over. It may have been over physically but certainly not emotionally. Where was all that anger hiding? It wasn't as if I felt it every day or even thought about it at all, but it was obviously there, somewhere. I thought since I was away from that environment, everything was fixed and I was okay. I had believed that part of my life was over, but I couldn't have been more wrong.

The abuse seemed to start when Jett entered puberty. He played pee-wee football, and from that time on, as long as he could exert his frustrations out on the field he left me alone. But, when he wasn't playing, there was hell to pay. He was a fast running-back and physically, much bigger and stronger than me. However, I was a faster runner. If I could get away from him, I was usually safe because he couldn't catch me. He continually barraged me with "sissy," "wimp," and "pussy." I really didn't care, because I didn't know what the words meant. I didn't think that my home life was any different from anybody else's. I thought everybody lived this way, and not knowing any different, I thought this was a normal brotherly relationship.

One particular afternoon after walking home from school, I wanted a glass of milk. Both of my parents didn't arrive home until about an hour after my sister, Jett and me. My oldest brother William had just entered the Marine Corps, so there was nobody home to keep the peace. When Jett heard me getting a glass from the cupboard, he decided to impose his authority over the situation.

What situation? Dirtying a clean glass, of course! He never washed a dirty dish in his life, but he insisted that I use a paper cup. When I refused, along with my older sister Ellen who was vouching in my defense, he proceeded to bash and punch both of us until we were able to break free. I ran next-door to Betty's house, who happened to be Jett's football coach's wife. I later discovered that Jett had beat the hell out of Ellen and blackened one of her eyes. From that moment on, I vowed to never claim him as my brother. I laid awake at night praying and wishing that he were dead. I began to hate him!

Jett didn't dare encroach on Coach King or his family because he knew there would be consequences on the football field. I thank God for Betty. She was there at the right place and time, providing that protection God knew I needed. She may not have known the circumstances were so dire, but God did. You see, even before I knew God, he was providing a safe place for me to go when I was in danger. Betty was standing in that gap created by Jett's abuse.

The abuse caused the gap. In other words, she created the gap that should not have been there or been allowed to develop. If Jett and I had been able to nurture a normal sibling relationship, the gap would not have been created. As the years progressed and the abuse continued to get worse, the gap widened. In fact, the gap eventually became so vast and destructive Jett and I had no communication at all and were totally and completely estranged as adults. We never spoke, called each other on the phone, saw each other at reunions, celebrated each other's successes, or comforted each other in disappointments. We didn't witness each other's families grow or share in God's blessing of children or prosperity. There was absolutely no relationship at all. The gap was final and absolute. I never felt any bonding, connection, or security in either of my brotherly relationships. I could never depend on him to "stick up for me" or defend me on the playground. I never felt assurance that he would be there if I needed him. I felt alone. I've wondered if it would have been better for me emotionally if he had never been a brother. William was so far removed from my experience that it was like he didn't even exist. And, the brother that was around was abusive. I would have been better off not to have had a brother because it only made me wish the relationship was more than it could be. I wouldn't have had the expectations.

As the abuse became worse, I built my walls higher. My resolve to defend myself welled up with great increase. My walls were in my mind and my heart. I felt isolated and abandoned by my parents. At first, I didn't understand why it was happening or why Mom and Dad weren't there to protect me. It felt as if they just didn't care. My father's denial of the abuse usually landed on my shoulders. It was always my fault. "Just ignore him" or "just walk away" was his standard response. It proved to take years for me to understand this approach and many more to forgive him. My mother's inability to control Jett was more readily understandable.

My mother was a strong-willed German woman. Staunch, robust, and full of life. I can still remember her boisterous laugh. You could find her in a crowded room simply by listening. I have many memories of her from when I was very young.

I had acute asthma as a toddler. Early my second winter, I can even remember her carrying me to the car in her arms, covered with a crocheted afghan to protect me from the cold air. We would play peek-a-boo through the holes in the shawl. I think my mother and I connected on a deeper level than my other siblings. She always encouraged my creativity and was my foremost teacher in life. She was a walking encyclopedia ready to disperse an answer to any of my questions.

My mother would often fix a large Sunday dinner for the family and invite the extended family. This was a perfect opportunity for Jett to demonstrate his tantrums. Many times the dinner ended up on the ceiling or all over the floor. He even dumped the Thanksgiving table one year. My grandfather, uncles, and cousins all tried to control him to no avail. Mom was the only one who could have any effect on him. Many times she would get him to the floor and sit on him. He would be so out-of-control, that a black look would come over his face, and a glazed look cloaked his eyes in rage. It looked as if Satan himself were alive. However, this approach didn't last long. Mom developed severe migraine headaches, which would completely incapacitate her. Her headaches became so debilitating that she would be bed ridden for days on end. She couldn't even keep her balance when she closed her eyes.

After many hospital tests, her doctors concluded that she had Degenerative Disk Disease and would need surgery on the discs between the cervical vertebrae in her neck. They performed two operations, taking chips of bone from her hip to fuse the vertebrae. We did not know then, but years of rehabilitation were required. The surgeries left her disabled and never completely alleviated from her symptoms.

My mother could no longer protect me. I had no choice but to build the walls even higher. I did everything I could to avoid Jett. I would go to a friend's house after school until I was certain that my father was home from work, even though I knew my mother needed me. Ellen and

I would lock ourselves in her room and only come out for dinner. I would play outside all evening until dark to avoid being near him. It became an endless game, which I often lost. To no avail, he would find a way to pick a fight, regardless of what I did or didn't do. *God, please protect me,* was all I could pray.

Soon, Will returned home on leave from the Marine Corp. He must have been bored one afternoon, so he recruited Jett to help perpetrate one of his cruel jokes. While Ellen and I were minding our own business, Will forced us to go out of the house onto the front yard. It so happened that we had a fire hydrant located in front of the house by the street curb. Without any physical force, he insisted that we sit back to back with the hydrant between us. We complied because he was one marine you didn't mess with. He then proceeded, with Jett's help, to tie us to the fire hydrant. In broad daylight—with no apparent objection from the neighbors. We sat there, tied with no chance of escape, waiting for our parents to return home from their errand. I could no longer trust either of my brothers.

Chapter 2

Why Hast Thou Forsaken Me?

But you, O God, do see trouble and grief;
you consider it to take it in hand.
The victim commits himself to you;
you are the helper of the fatherless.

Psalm 10:14 (NIV)

Psalm Chapter 10 is a very strong source of inspiration and hopeful trust in the Lord. And I must say that I do not view or interpret these scriptures lightly. I believe that all of us have a responsibility to the preservation and reverence of the Holy Scriptures. With that in mind, I would encourage you to read this particular Psalm for yourself. I also believe that all of the scriptures have a personal meaning to us for our situation and circumstances when we look for its applicability.

In Chapter 10 David is writing about how sometimes God appears to be distant or non-participatory when we face strife or affliction. As you read further into the Psalm, you can begin to detect that God is protecting us from afar or behind the scenes. As David pleads with the Lord to stop the unfairness of the boastful and wicked, he challenges the Lord to arise and stand up for the forsaken. He wants God to acknowledge that He sees the oppressors and the injustice that is inflicted upon the helpless and the poor in spirit.

Have you ever felt oppressed? Do you know, or are you at least familiar with, that deep discouraging feeling? Has anyone at work, or school, or even at church treated you like your opinion wasn't as good or right as theirs or that your experience wasn't as good as theirs? Did it make you feel inferior or not good enough? I believe this is what David is referring to but on a much deeper, broader, and damaging level. When this occurs I believe it cultivates a poor spirit. Depression, isolation, and sadness may be experienced. It may cause you to lose your confidence in yourself and your faith. Sometimes you may even feel helpless to fight it. Like your weapons against it have been taken away or destroyed. In Psalms Chapter 10 David is reminding us that our weapon is God. It is his rightness to protect His children. God can cover us with a cloak of rightness and confidence in Him. All we need to do is trust Him. He is our hope. He is our "general" if you will. He carries the arsenal and can shoot the weapons to defend us. He can command His angels to come to our defense if He chooses. In Daniel 3:28 Nebuchadnezzar praised God for sending His angel to rescue Shadrach, Meshach, and Abednego from the fire. So why doesn't He send His angels to rescue us? God does not want us to live in terror (Isaiah 54:14). Most of the time, He works behind the hidden scenes to advocate us. He cares about the forsaken and the forgotten. He certainly hears our prayers and cries.

Even though my mother was my protector, she also had a dark side. She maintained a very strict code of expectations for us. We were expected to tow the line no matter what, and do what we were told with no questions asked. At times, this nurtured the rebellion in me.

When I started kindergarten, I learned my first cussword. F***! My mother was furious. She drug me to the bathroom, removed all of my clothes, and spanked my bare butt with a belt. She then washed my mouth out with Zest soap. I still remember the taste. Not good. As I was cumbersomely working my shirt over my shoulders, I became entangled and frustrated, and blurted out "F***!" again. I endured the punishment ritual once more.

When I was ten, I started sneaking a smoke with the next-door neighbor. I was soon riding my bike to the grocery store and stealing packs of cigarettes. Of course, I wasn't very good at it, and I was soon caught by the store manager. As his punishment, I had to tell my parents and return to the store with them that evening to pay for the stolen merchandise. I did as I was told, and when we returned home, my mother instructed me to put my hands on the kitchen counter. I stretched my fingers out onto the counter. My mother proceeded to bend over and remove her high heeled shoes. I knew what was coming, and I started pleading with her not to do it.

"Are you ever going to steal again?" she demanded while her voice pitched higher.

"No! No! Please don't." I begged, crying before I ever felt a thing.

Strike! Then again, strike! Then again, strike! Ten times.

She didn't miss a finger. I never stole again.

By age twelve I thought God did not hear my cries any longer. I remember praying for God to strike Jett dead. I felt so much hate toward him and I no longer wanted to claim him as my brother. I just wanted God to takes him in his sleep, and if that didn't happen, I would think of ways I could kill him. I would think of different scenarios that allowed me to get away with taking his life. His constant torment was becoming unbearable. Why wasn't God answering me? Why wasn't He protecting me? I had learned in church that He loved children and didn't want any of us to suffer, so why was he letting Jett cause so much terror? And why was my earthly father letting this happen? I didn't understand why Dad was so silent and dismissive.

Every time an incident or fight would happen, Dad always blamed me. Even when the fight happened right in front of him, the fight was always my fault. Jett was blameless. I didn't understand it. I became bitter toward my father. He was not protecting me as I felt he should. I felt that I was deserving of his protection; he should be able to see the injustice of Jett's actions. I tried to rationalize it and figure it out. I mistakenly applied logic to something that was totally irrational.

I very seldom got into trouble. I earned wonderful grades and received numerous awards and accolades in school. It wasn't long before I noticed that my father was never there when I participated in something wonderful in school. Even when I was inducted into the Honor Society, he was absent. I never had a sense from him that he was even remotely proud of me. What did I have to do to receive his love?

There was one incident when I was about twelve years old that stuck in my mind for many, many years. My father and I had just had words about a situation with Jett. As I was marching up the stairs angry, I screamed, "I hate you." He replied, "I hate you too!"

I burst into tears and ran to my room. Shame and rejection had never hurt so bad or cut so deep. I was devastated. *Why did he hate me?* I couldn't help but ask myself, *Am I really that despicable? What was I doing wrong?* He always treated me like he could have cared less about me. He played ball with my brothers, but not me. I felt the sting of being forsaken. I was forgotten. *Why didn't he love me?* I thought God had forsaken me too. I wasn't worthy of an answer to my prayers.

But why doesn't God answer sometimes? Why does He let some things happen? I've asked myself this question a thousand times. I'm not sure that I fully understand the answer, but this is my take on it. *God wants us to learn to trust Him totally and completely.* Yes, I think it's that simple. It is in those deep despairing moments when we truly seek the Holy Spirit. It is in those moments when we truly seek His direction and understanding. He might not give the solution desired, or an answer that fits the expectation, but the answer that is given *is best.* It took twenty-one years for this to manifest a full circle in my life, but when the answers came . . . it was sooooo sweet!

My wrist was bleeding profusely. I was screaming and pounding on the front door. Jett had locked me out of the house. I had just put my hand through the garage door window, and glass was sticking out of my flesh. I was trying to stop my brother from massacring a toad with a firecracker. He was always doing something inhumane, and I just couldn't stand for it. He must have been deranged. Toad guts were all over the garage. Eventually, the neighbor across the street called the police, as she was always looking out of her living room window to see what was going on. Can you blame her? Jett certainly had a reputation in the neighborhood. My parents were away, taking Ellen to the airport for a flight to Nashville to meet her fiance's parents. Naturally, Jett had the opportunity to, once again, inflict pain and suffering.

The police arrived shortly after Jett had wrestled me to the concrete driveway and repeatedly jumped on my back and head. God must have sent an angel to protect me from permanent damage. Jett ran into the house, and the policeman immediately came to my rescue. He tended to the glass sticking out of my wrist and placed me in the back of the police car. I remember how hot it was that summer day. Jett was always worse in the summer because he didn't have anything to do. There wasn't any football to alleviate his frustration, so he took it out on something helpless and innocent. The officer went to the front door, which Jett had evidently locked and refused to answer, so the policeman returned to the car and started asking me what happened. He inquired who our family doctor was, and he called the dispatcher to arrange for immediate treatment. I remember sitting in the back seat of the cruiser feeling so scared I was numb. As we started to back out of the driveway, Jett appeared on the front porch insanely waving his fist in the air. Swearing, "Don't bring that bastard home, or I'll kill him!" We started down the street in front of my house, and all the neighborhood kids I played with were gathered, pointing at me as if I had done something tragic. I really don't remember much else, other than my doctor becoming very upset after speaking to the officer and waiting for what seemed to be forever to go home.

I knew what was waiting for me when I got there. The officer hung up the phone from speaking with my parents and proclaimed that he would take me home. I was glad that he would be there. I felt some sense of relief that at least he was on my side. Maybe Dad wouldn't be so angry at *me* after hearing the story from the policeman. We pulled into the driveway and my father was on the front porch. I hung my head, as I passed by him. I slipped through the front door, looked up, and spotted my mother in the kitchen directly in front of me. I heard Dad follow me into the foyer.

"I told you to stay away from him! See what happens?" Dad shouted.

The officer spoke up and explained that a neighbor had called the station and reported that a young boy was getting "beat-up" across the street. The officer moved into the kitchen, standing in the doorway behind Dad at attention. Just then, the front screen door burst open and Jett bounced through the hallway as if nothing had happened. The officer turned and locked eyes with Jett, causing him to instantly change his disposition.

"Would you like to explain yourself, young man?" the officer said.

"Not to you!" Jett replied.

"Then explain it to me!" Dad interjected.

Dad grabbed Jett by the front of his shirt, slammed him into the refrigerator and hit him square in the face. Jett's nose started to bleed. I could tell that Jett was stunned.

"I can see that you have things well under control, Mr. Lewis. I'll leave you now to settle this situation," the officer said, then turned to leave.

Yes! Yes! Yes! I was screaming in my mind. I couldn't believe what I just witnessed. My father actually defended me. Well, maybe he was just embarrassed by the policeman's involvement, but I didn't care. Justice had finally been done. Jett finally got what he deserved. Then a terrifying thought came, *How is Jett going to retaliate? Oh no!* I quickly retreated upstairs and locked myself into the bathroom. I stayed there until it was time for dinner. I thanked God for the officer who stood in the gap that day.

Chapter 3

Run For The Hills

Truly in vain is salvation hoped for from the hills,
and from the multitude of mountains;
truly in the Lord our God is the salvation of Israel.

Jeremiah 3:23 (KJV)

I don't know what made Jett fly into his tirades. I strongly believe now that he had a chemical imbalance. In those days medications weren't available, and child protection laws were virtually non-existent. Another option that my parents considered was to turn him over to The State of Ohio and have him committed to an institution. This was simply out of the question as far as my mother was concerned. Mom and Dad took him to numerous counselors and therapists, but Jett would never cooperate. He knew that as long as he didn't talk, eventually he wouldn't have to go any more. This placed the entire family in a defense mode, never knowing when he would explode.

My mother was home convalescing shortly after her first neck surgery. She would spend days in bed and only venture outside when it was absolutely necessary. She never went anywhere without a rigid plastic neck brace the doctor had prescribed. Her life had become an endless schedule of doctor appointments, migraine headaches, and pills. Ellen and I picked up most of the slack for things that needed to be done around the house. Ellen cooked most of the meals and did laundry. I cleaned bathrooms, ran the sweeper, and dusted. Jett did nothing, of course.

Late one afternoon when school was over, I was doing chores. Mom was convalescing from her first surgery, who was still bed-ridden. Jett accused me of having one of his shirts in my dresser drawer. I don't know why it was there—maybe Ellen had placed it improperly because she wasn't sure who it belonged to. But in Jett's world, I would have thought the sky was falling. It didn't dawn on him that I wouldn't be caught dead in anything he put on his body because I cared too much about how I looked. But that didn't stop him from throwing a tantrum. He proceeded in destroying my half of our shared bedroom. I tried to stop him but to no avail; he continued slamming drawers and throwing clothes all over the floor.

Mom heard the commotion and was soon standing at our door. By this time the arguing had escalated into fighting, and mom's sudden presence at the door gave me the opportunity to get away from him. I flew down the hallway and down the stairs. This infuriated Jett. The look of rage was masking his face, and Mom knew what his intentions were. She grabbed him by the back of his shirt as he tried to escape past her. She somehow got him to the floor on his back, and she sat on him. She would place a cold washcloth on his forehead. This was the only way she could get him to calm down. She could always tell from the look in his eyes when he was out of control.

It didn't matter this time. Mom was weak, and Jett knew it. He lunged his belly upwards and flipped her off his torso. The only problem was that they were at the top of the stairs, and mom went tumbling. She tried to stop herself by grabbing the wrought iron railing, but she continued to roll. She came to a rest in the foyer on the hard tile floor. Jett darted out the front door, quickly vanishing from sight. I peered from behind the adjacent wall and knelt by Mom's side. She was in tears. I don't know if the tears were from pain or from a broken heart. I helped mom back up the stairs and into bed. I did my best to tend to her. I didn't know what to do. I asked if she needed a doctor. She replied, No.

"What do you want me to do?" I asked.

"Just let me rest," she replied.

"Is your neck hurting?"

"No," she said.

I could tell from her voice that she was certainly distressed. I don't think she wanted me to call for an ambulance because she knew that it might be the last straw for my father. I stayed with her until Ellen came home. Years later, after my mother's death, I asked Dad about this incident. He never knew. He was stunned.

That summer Mom and Dad put the house up for sale. I really didn't want to move. I had just finished the eighth grade and was looking forward to my freshman year. I was very involved in the school chorus and had been encouraged by my music teacher to try out for a prestigious high school ensemble. I was accepted into this musical group that not only sang and performed but traveled to other schools and competed in state-wide competitions. I was psyched. Earlier in the school year, I had the privilege of participating in an opera. I had so much fun learning the music and participating in that spectrum of entertainment. I learned so much from professionals and truly wanted to explore the possibilities. But it wasn't to be. We were moving, and mom wanted to take Jett far away. He was spiraling out of control. I'm sure they thought something had to change.

Mom always wanted a house in the country on a hill surrounded by pine trees. After much searching, she found it, located in southeastern Ohio in the Hocking Hills region. It was located along a hilltop ridge outside a small village called Laurelville. Bittersweet and honeysuckle grew in abundance among the Sassafrass and Laurel trees. It was a small horse ranch surrounded by rolling hills and quaint country towns. The hills seemed to be alive with a renewed energy. A fresh start. I think mom felt better just being away from the bustle and tension of the city. I believe she found solace and peace among the pines. Even though conveniences were quite different and harder by far, the family seemed to settle into our new surroundings.

The house was much smaller, built by the previous owner. Constructed of rough-cut oak for the frame with clapboard siding, whitewashed, not painted, it appeared as though it had been added on to a couple of times. We only had one small bathroom. The kitchen floor slanted downhill, and running water was quite questionable, even on a good day. We had the well re-drilled and often times hauled five-gallon buckets of water from the cistern to the stove to be heated for bathing and dish washing. Not so much fun in the wintertime, but we adjusted. There was something about the fresh country air. The crisp scent of the pines, the surrounding landscape without neighbors, and the sloping hills with tall grass, all equaled a copasetic sense of contentment. It was as if the hills were protecting me, sending an inaudible signal of comfort. Rest, rest indeed.

O Lord, you have searched me
and you know me.

You know when I sit and when I rise;
You perceive my thoughts from afar.
You discern my going out and my lying down;
You are familiar with all my ways.
Before a word is on my tongue
you know it completely, O Lord.

Where can I go from your Spirit?
Where can I flee from your presence?
If I go up to the heavens, you are there;
If I make my bed in the depths, you are there.
If I rise on the wings of the dawn,
If I settle on the far side of the sea,
even there your hand will guide me,
your right hand will hold me fast.

If I say, "Surely the darkness will hide me
and the light become night around me,"
even the darkness will not be dark to you;
the night will shine like the day,
for darkness is as light to you.

For you created my inmost being;
you knit me together in my mother's womb.
I praise you because I am fearfully
and wonderfully made;
your works are wonderful,
I know that full well.

Psalm 139:1-14 (NIV)

I felt as though God was protecting me. He knew what I needed—what we all needed. He had everything under control and it didn't matter if I understood it or not. He was going to protect me. Many nights of prayer had been answered, and I consciously felt it. I was experiencing peace for the first time in my young life. I'm sure there were moments of it before but certainly not a sense of contentment overtaking my life. It felt good. It felt as though something good was happening, and God was going to take care of me.

School started. I hated the first day of school. I had to ride a school bus for the first time, which I never had to do in the city. I got on the bus that first morning and these provincial country bumpkins looked at me as if I had three heads. I guess I was different. I always primped my hair, wore clean pressed pants (not jeans) and dress shirts. Most kids were wearing overalls and flannel shirts (I didn't have any) and looked like they just came in from the barn. Maybe they did. 'Didn't matter to me; I just wanted to be liked. I just wanted to fit in.

The bus driver Thelma was an older lady who lived up the road. She had kids my age, but she became my new best friend. I don't know why she took me under her wing, but I sure appreciated it. She soon discovered that Jett liked to pick on me rather incessantly during our one-hour trips to and from school. This was so embarrassing and Thelma could tell. Many times I had to sit directly behind her to avoid his impingements.

Shortly after school started that year, Thelma received a new bus. It was bright and shiny with new comfortable seats. It even had a radio with satellite speakers so everyone could listen. What a treat and Thelma thought so too. Soon after it arrived, she told me to stop by her house and she would take me for a ride, just us. Oh, COOL! I couldn't wait. So, after school that day, I checked in with mom to gain her permission, then hurried up to Thelma's. We were soon tracking down the hills and curves that were so characteristic of the ridge that we lived on. Down the road a bit, Thelma said, "Hold on tight, I want to show you something." I braced myself in the seat behind her, gripping the cold chrome grab-pole behind her seat.

"Ready?" she said.

"Yes" I replied, not having a clue what I was preparing myself for. Suddenly, she stomped on the brakes. I could feel the momentum forcing me forward until the bus reached a complete stop almost instantly. "Wow!, How did it do that?" I asked.

"This bus is equipped with electronic brakes," she explained. She seemed to be so excited. I thought that it must have been the first time she had been given a new bus.

"Let those brats act up now!" she said.

I laughed.

It wasn't more than a few days later, Jett started it again. Was this ever going to end? He started picking on me early that morning. I don't remember why. It wasn't as if he ever needed a reason. By the time we both got on the school bus that morning, it was into a full-fledged fight. He was punching the back of my head as we trotted onto the bus. Thelma immediately came to my defense and insisted that he stop. I found my seat, and Jett landed two seats behind me. The other kids were always very quiet when Jett and I were fighting. I felt so embarrassed. I don't think most of them had ever been around someone like him. They were probably afraid to say anything. I wished someone would feel brave enough to stop him. Thelma tried to control him several times in the past by making him sit in the front seat, but this only infuriated him more.

But this morning was different. I looked up and saw Thelma watching us in her full-rear-view mirror. Jett kept leaning over the seat between us and slapping me in the back of the head, calling me names. I glanced up and saw Thelma smile at me. She caught my attention, but why was she smiling? Ah! I smiled back because I knew what she was going to do. I kept watching her, and she kept glancing up at her mirror. Just at the right moment, Jett raised and leaned forward to slap me in the head, Thelma slammed on her brakes, hard! Jett suddenly lurched forward, tumbling into the seat between us and onto the bus floor. The sound of his body hit the back of my seat with a THUMP! As he hit the floor, it made everyone on the bus gasp. The next thing I knew, everyone was laughing, pointing at Jett. He never picked on me again while Thelma was around. *Thank you Thelma for standing in the gap!* I liked Thelma very much. She made me feel grown up. Then I realized that I felt happy. I wasn't very familiar with that emotion. I liked it.

I was experiencing many new things. I enjoyed taking long walks in the woods. Observing the different trees, and the ferns that grew wild among the pines, and watching, and listening to the brook that flowed from a spring along our ravine. I loved tromping up and down the steep hillsides. I liked the smell of cut grass and the leaves in the fall. I liked spending hours just riding the lawn mower while cutting our three acres of yard. It was as if I was noticing these things for the first time. I was experiencing all of my surroundings, and it naturally started to heal me. And, although I liked the solitude of our new home, I was discovering that I was also making new friends. Jett was slowly fading into the background.

Chapter 4

He Knew Me

Thine eyes did see my substance,
yet being unperfect:
and in thy book all my members were written,
which in continuance were fashioned,
when as yet there was none of them.

Psalm 139:16 (KJV)

His eyes saw me. Imperfect, yet being formed. He fashioned me, made me, formed me, and knew me (Jer 1:5). My members are even recorded in a book (Ex 32:32, Rev 21:27). He has even kept track of every part of my body. God created all of heaven and earth (Gen 2:4), and yet he intimately knows every being ever formed, every life lived, and every thought and action taken and not taken. How great is the omnipotence of God that he could possibly know what I'm thinking and what is in my heart and soul (Ps 26:2).

He knows because He made us. He created the very atoms that make up the molecules, that make up the DNA, that make up the cells, that make the very tissues in our bodies. Those cells give us the ability to think, make judgments, and decisions. Thoughts that create ideas, understanding, and rationality (1 Tim 1:7). He also created

23

us in His image (Gen 1:27) with His very breath giving us life. Breath gives us life. We would die within minutes if we didn't breathe. Air is what we consume to sustain our body. Life is what we consume which sustains our souls. As we live and time passes, we use up our earthly life, and our souls naturally grow weary of living. Our spirits are eternal and live forever because God's breath gave our spirit life (Gen 2:7).

Our bodies are intricately formed, every cell made for its intended purpose and functioning according to a divine map. Even with the mapping of the human genome, scientists are still looking for the map legend or key that unlocks the intention of the very atoms that create the cells. How do they know what to do or what their intended purpose is? Every intricate blood vessel, nerve, brain synapse, protein, or enzyme has its reaction to some other component that *only it* reacts to. How does this happen, or come into existence? Evolution through millions of years? This can't possibly explain all of it. The variables are too numerous for chance. For example, just think about conception. What is it about a sperm cell that knows where to go, what to do, and how to do it. How does that chemical reaction cause the cells to grow and divide perfectly? What tells them to do that? The human body is the most extraordinary living organism ever known to be in existence. It didn't happen by chance.

I've never questioned that God made me. I've always accepted it and have known it to be true. I've known in my spirit (the part of me that knows I think and can observe myself), that a divine power created me and communes with me. There have been times when I've listened to His direction and guidance and times when I have not. There are times when I can feel Him touch me in a very physical way. It starts at the top of my head and gently flows down my shoulders and back. Sometimes it is so strong I can feel it down to my toes. Sometimes it makes the hair on my arms stand erect, and other times His touch makes me cry. All of these sensations I count as God communicating with me. If I'm quiet and expecting to hear His voice, I can discern when He speaks. If the information that is communicated is good, or for my benefit, I know that it is God. This may be oversimplifying it a bit, but I think we are all made in this manner. In other words, He *knows* me.

God made me and He loves me just the way I am. I realize it now, but when I was a teenager, I'm not sure that I fully understood God's love. I thought that God loved me based on my actions. My understanding was that His love was conditional, based upon doing things right and being good. Perfect behavior is impossible for us as humans, but it was not my thinking then. I felt tremendous shame when I did something wrong. I felt alone and troubled because I had let someone down. If I didn't get good grades in school, I thought I had disappointed my parents. If I got in trouble or acted out, I felt disgust for myself. I was continually trying to mask my real feelings and portray a normal undamaged person. I didn't want anyone to see my real emotions or feelings because I thought they were ugly and dirty. I had feelings of which I was unsure. They were sexual, homosexual to be exact.

Every time I came across an article in a magazine or *Reader's Digest* about homosexuality, I read it and couldn't absorb enough of the information. I was always curious. Always secretly inquiring. I was sure it must be kept a secret, because I knew boys were supposed to like girls, but I didn't feel that way at all. I knew it wasn't acceptable and should be kept hush-hush. In my quietness, I fantasized about the male body, the embrace of strong arms, but kept it behind my private wall so that nobody else would see. I began to notice that the scent of a male made me aroused. *Why was this happening? Was this normal? Who could I ask without being ashamed of myself?* I thought that I would surely have to keep this secret no matter what. *I could never tell another soul. Never share it. How do I figure this out? Do I need to do something about it?* I thought about this dilemma for a long time, looking for a way to feel good about myself. I needed someone to boost me up, tell me that I was special, loved, and wanted. Unfortunately, I didn't get that from my family, and God was keeping silent.

I knew of God from going to church every Sunday while growing up, but I still didn't *know* Him. I felt Him in my life, but I didn't have a personal relationship with Him. I believe this is what is referred to as Providential Grace (Ps 32:7-8). This is when God kept His hand on my life, even though I did not yet let His spirit into my heart (1 John 3:4). His extension of protection over me kept me on the path that later brought me to a full knowledge of His forgiveness, or being "saved". Even though I knew God wanted this for me, I had not yet asked Him into my heart. I had not yet experienced His complete and unconditional love (1 John 4:16-17). In fact, I didn't even have a concept yet that He could love me so much, or that His love would cover me, so that I was blameless in His sight. I didn't know that He loved me just the way I was.

Shortly after school started that freshman year, Jett brought home a friend he had met in one of his classes. His name was Donny. When he entered the kitchen where I had been helping Mom prepare dinner, I turned to greet him, and I think I stopped breathing. He was incredibly attractive. He had flowing brown hair, high cheek bones, and a square jaw. He was slightly taller than me, but when his brown-eyed gaze met mine, he seemed to look right through me. I don't think I said much because I was embarrassed inside. I tried to conceal it, but I sensed that he knew.

After dinner we sat around the table and conversed. Mom and Dad were curious about Jett's new friend; after all, Donny had his drivers license and they needed to know if they could trust him. But they weren't as curious as me. Letting him look directly into my eyes again couldn't happen, then he would know for sure.

I soon left the table and stepped out onto the front porch. I loved gazing up at the stars. They were so plentiful and bright up on that dark hill. Soon Jett and Donny were making plans to go to another friend's house. When they were getting ready to leave, Donny stepped out onto the front porch and found me sitting on the edge of the front stoop.

He instantly said, "Next time you find yourself alone, give me a call and we can do something."

I was silent as he handed me a piece of paper with his phone number on it. I slid it into my pocket before Jett came out the front door. I mustered up the courage to reply, "okay."

The next day I passed Donny in the hallway between classes at school. For a brief second our eyes met again. He had the same look on his face as he did when I met him the night before. It was a gaze that seemed to say something, and even though I was only fourteen, I knew what that "something" meant. I sat through my math class with an erection just thinking about him. *Stop That!* I kept telling myself. I couldn't concentrate on anything but him. Every time I looked at my homework on the desk in front of me, I saw his handsome eyes.

A couple of days had passed when I arrived home and found that Mom was gone. She left a note saying she was in Columbus and wouldn't be home until late. "Go ahead and fix yourself a sandwich" she wrote. "Love You, Mom."

Jett was at football practice and Dad was picking him up after work. I quickly thought of Donny and wondered what he was doing. I went to my bedroom and found his phone number.

"Hello, is Donny there?" I asked.

"This is Donny," a voice returned.

"This is Jon, remember me, Jett's brother?"

"Hey, what's going on?" he asked.

"I was wondering what you were doing. Everyone is gone and I'm here by myself," I said.

"I can be there in twenty minutes," he replied.

"Great, see you in a bit." I hung up the phone. I was nervous. *Was there anything to this?* I wondered.

Donny soon arrived in his brown 1963 Chevy Bellair. He got out of his car, and I noticed that his swagger was confident and nonchalant. He immediately extended a grasp to my shoulder and asked what I wanted to do. I didn't offer any ideas, so he suggested that we run into town to get a bite, I could spend the night, and he would take me to school the next day. I agreed, wrote mom a quick note to let her know my plans, and grabbed some clothes for school the next day. I knew that mom probably wouldn't let me since it was a school night, but she couldn't stop me since she wasn't there.

We did the normal burger thing, then Donny took me to a lake near his house where he often went fishing.

"Do you like to fish?" he asked.

"I don't know. I've never done it."

"Didn't your dad ever take you fishing?" he asked

"Never"

"Well, you ought to try it sometime. You never know what you might catch," he said as he looked at me with a cheesy grin.

"I think it's boring, just sitting there, don't you?" I asked.

"But there's a lot that you can do that *is* interesting, if you know what I mean," he answered.

"What?" I replied, knowing full well what he meant.

It was starting to get dark so we headed to his house. I met his parents, who seemed largely disengaged and disinterested. Oh well, I thought. Donny had two younger brothers, but since he was the oldest, he had his own bedroom. Donny offered me his bed, as he pulled a sleeping bag from his closet and proceeded to unroll it onto the floor next to the bed. He started unbuttoning his shirt while I fumbled with my duffle bag, stalling for time. I didn't want to get undressed until he did. I felt totally embarrassed, but he flipped off the light before he removed his pants. I removed all of my clothes and slipped under the covers. The room was totally dark until my eyes adjusted to the ambient moonlight coming through his open bedroom window. The fall air was crisp, gently moving the curtains. I lay still for a very long time, listening for any sound that Danny made. My mind was racing, anticipating, hoping for something, anything. Out of the silence Danny spoke.

"This floor is so hard."

"There's plenty of room up here," I said, jumping on the opportunity just to be close to him.

"Are you sure?"

"Yea," I said.

Donny lifted the covers and settled next to me. I could feel his warmth even though he wasn't touching me. *What next? Do I dare say something.* I laid there quiet and still. Several moments passed.

"Are you thinking what I'm thinking?" he asked.

I was instantly aroused. I knew what he was thinking, and I wanted him to touch me.

"I don't know, what are you thinking?" I stupidly answered.

"Never mind."

A moment passed as I mustered the courage to engage him.

"I probably am," I said.

I couldn't believe it came out of my mouth. The next few moments seemed to last forever. Every detail is permanently etched in my mind. I felt the back of his hand brush against my upper thigh.

"Oh, you don't have on any underware!" he stated.

"No, I sleep in the nude," I said.

He quickly lifted his covers and rustled off his shorts. Just then, I felt his hand touch my chest ever so gently. I took a deep breath as his hand softly paused on my belly. This was intense. My breathing became heavy, almost laborsome. I had never felt so aroused in the past when I would please myself. He continued to softly massage me as I reached for him. I touched his belly as I felt it flinch. He had very soft hair around his navel.

"It's okay!" he said interrupting any further comment.

The aroma was sweet. He raised slightly and met my lips. I could tell that he hadn't shaven and his stubs were bristly. He opened his mouth, and I could feel his warm tongue. We embraced for what seemed like hours. It was welcoming. It felt safe, accepting, loving, and satisfying.

The next morning I woke from what little sleep I had managed. Donny's warm body was next to me. I glanced at his alarm clock, and it was 5:17 A.M. I lay there touching his belly and he stirred. He raised his head to look at the alarm clock. He stated that we better get a jump on getting ready for school before his brother's woke. He sprang out of bed, and I could barely see his silhouette before his slipped on his robe. I could still smell him next to me as he left the room to take his shower. The scent of his hair still lingered on the pillow as the warmth from his body was quickly fading. I didn't want the night to end. I was exhilarated and spent at the same time.

The morning air was damp and cold. Donny unlocked my door, then quickly turned towards his side of the car. The windshield was frosted and the car had a difficult time starting. As I sat on that cold seat, waiting for the car to warm, I watched Donny scrape the windshield. I couldn't help but think back on the night. I felt connection.

After a cold drive, we arrived at school. We were both walking down the hallway at school, and I noticed the burn on my cheek from his whiskers. When we separated to go to our lockers, he stopped first then fiddled with his combination lock. I kept walking, not saying a word. A few more feet, I turned around to steal one more glance. He was watching me. I smiled.

Chapter 5

The Vision

And it shall come to pass that I shall pour out my spirit upon all flesh; and your sons and daughters shall prophesy, your old men shall dream dreams, your young men shall see visions.

Joel 2:28 (KJV)

I liked my new life. I enjoyed my new friends. And even though we lived in what felt like the middle of nowhere, I liked that too. By chance, my aunt and uncle knew a family down the road from us who raised and sold Arabian horses. Everybody in the area knew Bo, and coincidentally, Thelma informed me she was looking for a hired hand. I asked my parents if this was something I could do after school. They approved, and arranged a meeting. Bo was delighted to have me work two to three hours per day cleaning the stalls, stabling and feeding the horses, and brushing them down. I was thrilled. I had always loved horses but knew nothing about them. Bo was cool with this and agreed to teach me about equine care and riding.

It wasn't long before Dad wanted one of the horses Bo had for sale. She was an expecting mare. I was excited to think that we would have a horse giving birth on the farm. Dad was soon building fences and stalls in our barn. After a few weeks we were ready to accept Topsy into our family. She was an older mare with a Quarter/Arabian mix. In fact this would probably be her last foal, which we were all anticipating. In the meantime Ellen and I convinced my father to let each of us purchase an Arabian yearling. We had the facilities to house two more. Also, Bo accepting my labor as payment made it even more feasible. The deal was done and we soon had three horses on our farm.

I learned a lot from Bo. She taught me how to train my gelding, Sandy. She taught me many important instruction techniques. I was soon working Sandy, and Ellen was training her horse Shane, on the weekends. It was great having a living, breathing responsibility. I could spend hours in the barn and corral with him. It seemed to tap into a place in me that I didn't know existed. Many hours were spent grooming, cleaning, watering, feeding, and training my new pride and joy.

It was easy to enthrall myself with my horse. Watching him grow was amazing, and I connected with him in a sense that I had never experienced before. There was something mystical when I stared into his eyes. I felt a sense of belonging or grounding, like I was supposed to be there for that experience. He taught me to care about the future. He taught me to trust in myself, and I soon felt something completely new: confidence and trust. Trusting him was easy because he trusted, and depended upon me.

But in sharp contrast I realized that I had difficulty trusting people. I couldn't discern what people's motives were, but with Sandy, I knew he had none. There was a pure heart, a primal instinct in him that I related to. Horses live in a constant state of fear, and when he was scared, I could immediately sense why. I could tell when he was happy and playful. I loved watching him run. It was like watching freedom explode but within limits. Something I longed for. Freedom to explore, to feel love, to be accepted, to be wanted, and to be nurtured. The fences held him in, but I could still feel my walls fencing me in. I longed to be like Sandy. Free. Maybe free from myself. Maybe free from expectation and rules. Maybe free from my desires.

Early that next spring, we were surprised to find that Topsy had delivered her foal. Bo had informed us that she would not let humans near when she delivered, so we erected more fencing for access to the wooded part of our property.

I woke early before school and went to the barn to feed and water the horses, as I did every day. It had become a normal routine for me, although, not an easy one that first winter. The air was cool, and I could see my breath. I glanced into the corral on my way to the large sliding barn door, and I noticed Topsy standing in the farthest corner. Wait, I saw more than four legs. I quickly ran back to the house to announce the news. She presented her newborn, which couldn't have been more than a few hours old, but was careful not to bring her foal too close. At first we couldn't tell if it was a male or female; she was very protective, always stepping in our path to position herself between us and the foal. After a few hours she became more tolerant of our presence, letting us inspect her new arrival. The vet was notified, and he gave the filly a thorough inspection. She was in fine health. His instructions for care were specific and well appreciated. This certainly was a new experience for us.

This new birth prompted me to think about children. To be more specific, my children. No, I didn't have any, as I was only fifteen, but knew I would at some point in the future. I did wonder what it would be like to be a parent. What it would be like to have a child; to know its name or what it would look like. I truly wanted to be a father someday. I wanted to experience that feeling, that belonging and attachment, that sense of creation. To know another being came from your own flesh. How incredible it must feel. I wondered whether I would have a son or daughter, or both, or many, or any. What was my future going to hold? I knew somehow I would be a father; I just didn't know how or when.

A year had passed since Topsy gave birth. The foal was named "Sundance" because she was born in the early morning when the sun first danced in the sky upon the tree tops. She was something to watch when she ran, kicking up her hind-hocks, flirting with the wind. She was full of "dance". My heart was full of song. I was joyful and enjoying my life for the first time.

Jett and I rarely fought anymore. He was busy working in Columbus at a bakery after school every day and was only home on rare occasions. After he earned his drivers license, I hardly saw him. It was a good thing. I had the house and the farm mostly to myself. Will was there occasionally when he was home on leave from the Marine Corp. My sister would visit most weekends with her fiance'. We would go horseback riding and hiking and visiting nearby forest parks. Mom and Dad would have bonfires in the fall. We saved cleared brush and fallen tree limbs and let them accumulate throughout the year. We would invite family and friends for an evening of singing, smores, and hayrides. It was a very good time in my life. A time for growing up, growing out and thinking about the future.

I was alone in my bedroom late one evening. Mom and Dad were in the living room watching television, and I was listening to my favorite pop group on my stereo. I was using my earphones, as not to disturb anyone, when I started to fall asleep. But it really wasn't sleep. It was that moment between sleep and awake, when everything seems suspended. Only this time it was different. It seemed to last a very long time. I was conscious but unaware of my body. I knew where I was but did not feel connected to anything. I was in a place unfamiliar to me, similar to someplace I knew, but nowhere specific. I looked downward toward my feet, and I saw a young boy; about three or four years old. He had light brown hair with a familiar face, similar to boyhood pictures, but not me. Then, in the very next moment, I saw this same boy but older; about fifteen or sixteen. I knew it was the same child, and this time I saw his face clearly. It was a version of me in the future, but not me. I saw his hazel eyes, like mine; his short thick brown hair, unlike mine. I looked more carefully and noticed that he had my nose and my bone structure. His frame was like mine was now, slim but shorter. His eyebrows were thick but shaped like mine. His complexion was olive-like and deep like mine. Then I saw his soul, and I knew that he was my son. At that moment I heard a noise outside my bedroom door and the captured moment was lost. I was suddenly brought to the present. I was profoundly dumbfounded. I knew, that I knew, that I knew, it was my son. I was sure beyond any doubt that I would have a son, my firstborn. What a revelation. I was excited and befuddled at the same time. What an awesome experience. God showed me something to secure myself in my future. I actually saw the future. *How can that be?* But, it happened. I saw it. I firmly believed it to be true and it would happen someday. I didn't know when, or by whom, but I knew it to be true.

Sons are a heritage from the Lord,
Children a reward from Him.

Psalm 127:3 (NIV)

I didn't learn of this scripture until many years later, but when I read it, I was prompted to remember the vision I had of my son. Webster's says that a "heritage" is property that descends to an heir; something transmitted or acquired from a predecessor; something possessed as a result of one's natural situation or birth (birthright). So, using this interpretation, God imparted my son to me (his heir), rightfully and naturally providing my heir. My son, my heir, is my reward from God. When my son was born, I remembered this promise from God and I blessed him. God keeps His promises. God keeps His children.

I believe we see visions at certain crossroads in our lives, if we pay attention to them and are open to their impressions. I believe that it really is common. God does communicate with us in many different ways. I wasn't looking for this particular one, but I believe God gave it to me as *a hope* for the future. I guess you could say that it *stood in the gap* at a time when I needed it. It showed me that even though I knew I was attracted to males—and being with a male was where my desire was—I was still going to father a child.

During this timeframe, I became very interested in drawing. I elected an industrial drawing class at school and discovered that I had a natural talent for engineering and drafting. I liked focusing on my work. It led me to a place of complete isolation, some refer to this as "the zone". Everything in existence around me would become invisible. Yes, I could still see, if I directed my attention away from my work, but my focus of concentration was so great that it blocked out everything else. Even my thoughts were totally and completely centered on what I was doing. It was a place of peace and contentment. A place that was quiet and secure. I only had to worry about what my hands were doing, or the math that was in my head. I would focus on the numbers and the math involved in the dimensions of my drawing. I would intently concentrate on how my fingers were forming the lines with my mechanical pencil. Only the piece of paper and I existed, and I was the creator of what was on that paper. It became very rewarding for me, and I became a master at this art very quickly.

During my sophomore year in high school, I had the opportunity to sign up for a vocational school. I was recommended by my drafting teacher. It was a two-year Engineering Graphics program at a nearby career training center. This program studied architectural and mechanical drafting along with associated state educational requirements. I discussed my transfer with Mom, and she thought that it would be a good opportunity for me. I completed the paperwork and mailed it in. I was accepted. I became very excited. This was a very important step in my training for a permanent career after graduation. I had given consideration to Ohio State University with a concentration in architecture; although, the large university scared me. I still had the option of college after this vocational program, and I considered it a head start. I thought it would secure my future.

Chapter 6

A Time For Testing

We set the wedding date for August first, two months after graduation. We were young, only eighteen, but we didn't care. We were in love and nobody was going to stop us. We were looking forward to graduation, and it was such a busy time of year, but we were both ecstatic about our future together.

I was fortunate to have found a drafting job through a recommendation from my Engineering Graphics instructor. I was making very good money by most standards back then—almost as much as my father. The last several months of school were extremely busy. I would go to school in the mornings to meet the state requirements then drive twenty miles to my new job. Metal fabrication was teaching me a great deal at a tremendous pace, and I loved it.

Mona was doing volunteer understudy work in dental offices wherever she could find it. She was required to have a certain number of hours completed to graduate from her Diversified Health Occupations program. Dentists in our geographical area were not willing to pay much nor were they very empathetic to mentoring young students. She told me of many instances when old, staunch dentists would become completely insultuous if she did not complete a task to perfection. But, she persisted, and it drove her to become a better person. Her persistence paid off; she was at the top of her class when she graduated.

We met our junior year at the vocational school. Across the hall from my drafting lab was a plethora of young ladies studying health occupations. They all wore cute little pink uniforms, their hair all tied up in buns or ponytails and white shoes. I was glad I didn't have to wear a uniform. No Thanks!

I never paid much attention to the girl who sat across from me because she always had her hair in one of those tight little buns, like a librarian. Then one day, I noticed that all the "pepto girls" (that's what we called them) were out of uniform and wearing normal clothes. They didn't have their hair tied back; they even wore make-up. I sat down at my desk in English class, looked over next to me, and beheld a beauty that I had never seen before. She had long, flowing dark brown hair that curled around her adorable little face. She had eyelashes that could have been wings and the cutest little nose. *Where did she come from?* She hadn't been there before. I certainly would have noticed. I asked for her name, and she replied, "Mona". Then I asked her if she had always sat there.

She replied, "yes," then she giggled.

"Don't remember me, do you?"

"Sorry, but no," I replied.

She giggled again.

The teacher started class, and I was completely taken back by her. *How did I miss this one,* I thought. She was very pretty. She was also very confident and forward.

After class she asked me out. I was so shocked and had such a shy nature, so I turned her down.

Later that same month, my best friend Bruce came to me and wanted to know what I thought about the girl across the hall whose name was Mona. He said he wanted to ask her out. I told him to go for it. He did, and they started dating. I was seeing Katy, a former classmate of Bruce's. So, when the Sweetheart Dance for Valentine's day approached, we all double dated to Bruce and Katy's home school. To make a boring story short, Mona and I ended up dancing most of the evening together.

I remember our first slow dance; she asked me out to the dance floor and wrapped her arms around me tight. She started grinding her hips against mine, and I didn't know what to think. *What was she doing?* When the dance was over, she kissed me. "Stop! No! No! No. You're Bruce's girlfriend!" I injected.

I couldn't do that to him. That was not cool. I hoped Bruce didn't see. I was suddenly uncomfortable. We went back to our table. It was obvious that Bruce hadn't seen, but Katy did. We quickly left, and Katy broke up with me the next day. I tried to explain, but she didn't care to listen. Bruce soon discovered what had happened; then, Mona broke up with him. I felt terrible about how things happened.

Feeling terrible didn't last long, as Mona and I were soon dating. Bruce stayed mad at me for a while, but he soon forgave me and we were friends again.

It wasn't long before Mona wanted me to meet her parents. I followed her home after school. I was nervous to say the least. We walked up to the front door and she unlocked it with her keys. We stepped into the foyer, and her father was the first thing I saw. Standing erect and seemingly displeased, he offered a very stern, "Hello".

I didn't quite know how to take him. Mona's mother, on the other hand, was very warm and friendly towards me. She offered the sofa for a comfortable seat, and we started chatting. She was soon learning all about my family with very cordial, non-threatening questions. I liked her. Her face was warm and her expressions non-assuming. I felt as if I'd known her for a very long time. She invited me to stay for dinner, and I could tell that Mona was pleased.

Mona's father, however, was difficult to figure out. He was blue collar. An obvious hard worker from the grease stains on his overalls and rough textured hands. He had obvious and genuine complete love for Mona. It was very evident that this was "his" little girl. He doted over her with great care as any proud father would. Although he spoke to her with gentle inflection in his voice, the same could not be said when he spoke to me. He was gruff and direct with a slight sense of intimidation. His face was aged, lips protruding from obvious lack of teeth, and silvering hair. He walked with a slight hunch but sure footed. I could tell that this man was the salt of the earth and worked hard to provide for his family. By the end of the evening, I believe I actually heard him laugh. I felt welcomed. I knew they were good people.

Mona and I said our goodnights in the driveway. I could feel eyes upon me, but I didn't dare look; I just behaved accordingly. She leaned toward me for a kiss, and I obliged. I drove home thinking about the evening and Mona. I was quite taken, but not smitten. I didn't know how to handle this girl; who was interested by all indications but somewhat forward for my experience. I left it to chance.

As time went by Mona and I became closer. She was interested in me—nothing I possessed or offered. She wanted to know about my family and especially my relationship with Jett. We spent many hours conversing about him and my experiences. She was empathetic, and I liked that. She displayed all of the emotions and concerns that made me feel special. I was vulnerable to her, I trusted her, I wanted her empathy. I wanted her to understand the abuse, and I wanted her to see that I was stronger than the sum of many years of torment. I wanted her to see me as a whole person, not damaged or victimized. I wanted her to feel confident that I wasn't verbally or physically abusive. I certainly didn't want to pass it on to her, and deep down I instinctively knew how not to do that. Many times a battered person extends this behavior to the ones he loves. I never felt that need or urge. I didn't possess that instinct or tendency. Somehow God gave me the ability to prevent it or bypass it. I would never hurt her, and I think she believed in me.

We spent the summer between our junior and senior years becoming closer. I remember driving home late one night after an evening together. We went to a drive-in movie, probably a horror flick; we saw a lot of those. I was driving my father's Volkswagen Beetle, and a song came over the radio. It was "Evergreen" by Barbra Streisand. As I listened to the words, tears welled up in my eyes and gently flowed down my cheeks. I was thinking about Mona and how much I had grown to love her. Her love felt comfortable and safe, even though it was completely terrifying to me.

I was trying to push other attractions out of my mind. I refused to think about Donny or any of the nights we spent together. I was determined to focus on my future with Mona and do what was right. Those other times were foolish and childish; I had no room for them in my life anymore. I wanted to choose the right path for my future and raise a family someday. I was beginning to believe that this was my chance. I thought that loving Mona could fix that defective part of me.

The fall of that year came quickly. My seventeenth birthday was approaching, and I was seriously considering asking Mona to marry me after we finished school, maybe sometime the following summer. I wanted her to know that I was serious and that I was ready for a permanent commitment.

I hatched a plan to surprise her on my seventeenth birthday, but the surprise was on me. Little did I know that she had managed to give me a surprise birthday party, at her house with most of my family there. After all the birthday wishes and surprises, I took her into a private room. I pulled out a small box, knelt to one knee and asked her to marry me. She immediately burst into tears and said, "Yes". It couldn't have been a more perfect time to share the news with the families. Although she hid it very well, I could sense that my mother was not pleased.

We were soon planning our wedding for August first of that coming summer. We spent the next few months planning, confirming our guests lists, meeting with the pastor of Mona's church; we bought dresses, shoes, candles, napkins and many other novelties for the wedding and reception. Pastor Black was very supportive and complimented that we both were very mature, approaching marriage with respect and confidence in each other. We had not yet turned eighteen, but Pastor Black thought we would be successful in our marriage because he could sense how in love and determined we were. He never mentioned that we would not be able to qualify for a marriage license due to the fact that the State of Ohio law required that both parties be eighteen unless the female was pregnant, regardless if parents were willing to sign consent. Mona didn't turn eighteen until September, and my birthday was in November. Ooops!

Mona's mother discovered this little tidbit from her best friend and confirmed it to be true. She informed me over the phone but had not yet told Mona. I asked her not to tell Mona until I could get to their house. I arrived shortly before Mona came home after work. She could sense that something was wrong as soon as she stepped into the house. I took her into her bedroom and broke the news. She immediately started crying. Her heart was broken. The disappointment was overwhelming for both of us. We consoled each other and promised each other to make this situation work. We vowed that this testing was just that, testing. A test we could face head-on together. We would just have to postpone the wedding until after my birthday. No big deal! We discussed a new date for November.

Chapter 7

The Spoiled Plan

Therefore shall a man leave his father and his mother,
and shall cleave unto his wife;
and they shall be one flesh.

Genesis 2:24 (KJV)

"Please make yourself comfortable. Sit back and relax. Clear your mind of all thoughts—at least as clear as you can. Try not to think about anything else but what I am telling you in the present. Concentrate on how you feel in your body. Your breathing, inhale-exhale, inhale-exhale. Softly listen to your breathing and be conscious of your chest rising and falling. Relax your mind even further. Relax to almost a sleep, but keep your mind conscious and awake. Let your body slip into a state of just existence. Let yourself feel comfortable with this state of relaxation."

"Now, I want you to imagine . . .", Oh wait! I can't remember all of it. Just bits and pieces.

I'm in a cave with my Grandfather. I am protecting him from a bear. It's dark, unfamiliar, deposing. What am I doing? Why am I thinking this? What is the purpose of all this?

The psychiatrist brings me back to the present and away from my psycho-hypnosis. I slowly wind down and come back to reality. He ends our session, leaving me with a very uneasy feeling, and I soon join my mother in the waiting room. I just wanted to forget the whole experience. *Why am I here anyway?*

My mother insisted that I see a psychiatrist after Mona and I were engaged. I couldn't quite discern whether she felt threatened by our engagement, or if she really thought something was wrong with me. In any case I wasn't going back, and she would just have to deal with it. I couldn't fit the pieces together and she never gave me an explanation. This placed a prolonged strain on our relationship to the point I would no longer confide in her. I stopped asking her permission to drive into town to see Mona; I just did it. I stopped coming home by curfew. I stopped eating meals with my parents and started spending more and more time at Mona's parent's house, which they welcomed.

My future mother-in-law and I became closer and closer. She didn't understand why my mother was being so obstinate. I understood that part; she didn't want me to marry, but I didn't understand what the psychiatrist was all about. Did she think I was crazy because I chose to marry Mona instead of going to college? In fact, she even went so far as to arrange a meeting with a local judge (under the pretense of usurping the law to allow us to marry), so that the judge could convince me to go to college instead. I found this manipulation deplorable. I was not going to accept or tolerate this kind of behavior from her. *I'll show her!*

Mona and I found an apartment, and I moved out of my parents house. Mona's father gave me a car so I could travel to and from school and work. Mona and I started working, cleaning and painting so it would be ready when it was time to move in. I slept on the sofa at my future in-laws house, while Mona and I put our future plans together.

It was in an old boarding house with maybe six apartments in the building. It was charming and had a lot of character but not much room. The kitchen was small and the one bathroom was even smaller. You could sit on the commode, brush your teeth, and take a shower all at the same time. But it soon became our home. We purchased a few pieces of furniture on time payments and family members gave us other necessities. We were on our way to becoming self sufficient. It wasn't easy, but in retrospect, it was very easy compared to today's challenges for young couples. Imagine a seventeen-year-old getting an apartment today.

Graduation came and went. My parents didn't make much of a deal over it; even though I graduated with honors, top of my class in Engineering Graphics with many accolades and awards. It didn't make me feel very special; in fact I was almost embarrassed because my parents were so unimpressed. It became obvious to me that I couldn't please them, so I turned my focus to our upcoming wedding. It was time for me to focus my attention on the love that I was receiving.

After an exceptionally hot summer we began preparing for the fall. My horse required hay to be put up for the winter. This was a yearly chore that I dreaded. It was so much work, as we needed to purchase and load the hay on the truck then unload the hay into the barn. It was a hot, sticky, itchy, exhausting task but needed to be done when the harvest came in. After we finished Mom would have our annual bonfire gathering. She always invited both sides of the family, friends, and neighbors. We would sing old songs and ride the hay wagon with the tractor. We also played hide-n-seek or threw the Frisbee or played volleyball.

This particular year, Mona and I were looking forward to our wedding. It was "the" topic of conversation. I had decided to let bygones be bygones (since we hadn't fought in long while) and ask Jett to be my best man. Before I could have a private conversation with him, he decided to have one with me.

I had gone into the house to use the bathroom when he confronted me in the hallway as I was leaving. His problem this time was the fact that Dad was forced to take care of my horse since I had moved out of the house. He didn't know I had plans of selling Sandy, but that didn't matter to him. I voiced my lack of concern for his opinion, which he didn't like much, because his next action was to shove me from the front porch causing me to fall to the ground. Mona was standing nearby talking with family and immediately came to see what was causing the argument. When I arose from the frontyard she stepped between us. I couldn't believe what she did; it was either stupid or brave, I wasn't sure which. Didn't she understand that he would hit her just as easily as he would me? Urgently, I gave Jett a very stern and certain warning not to touch her. I think he knew that I meant business because he backed up. By this time Dad appeared and told us to break it up. Jett stormed off, got into his car, and left. I was so relieved that he didn't try to strike Mona. The adrenaline was rushing through my body. Mona saw firsthand what he was really like. I thanked her and told her to never do that again. I couldn't believe I was stupid enough to think he would be in my wedding.

I was having second thoughts. Where was God in all of this? Why was He being silent? I didn't have any sense of direction. Was I making the right decision? I knew I had these homosexual feelings in me and hoped if I ignored them and kept them behind my protective walls, it would be safe. I was hoping that it would never hurt Mona. I couldn't help but doubt myself. Was this confusion being caused by Jett? I couldn't discern the right thing to do. I couldn't tell. Was I making the right decision to marry Mona. I thought I would have some kind of confirmation from God. If I did the wrong thing, I would hurt a lot of people and God; I surely didn't want that. But which choice was right? Marry the girl I loved and hope that it fixes me, or be honest with myself and trust something totally uncertain? *God, where is your voice?*

I contemplated telling Mona about my homosexual escapades. I didn't know how she would react to the news. I couldn't predict her response. Would she understand, or would she freak out and break up with me? I spent a lot of time thinking through each scenario. I knew that she had a right to know, but if marriage fixed me, no harm would be done. I decided that it would not help her in any way to understand this part of me since I was leaving it in the past. I had no plans of acting upon my attractions or hurting Mona. That was the last thing I wanted to do. I believed that after we were married and my sexual needs were being met and would stop feeling this attraction to men and I wouldn't have any further need to fantasize about being with a man. Mona would be all I would need. I wanted her to be all I would need. I wanted that deep intimacy with her that was so connecting and personal. I wanted to possess what I saw in other couples.

The big day had come! I arrived at the church early as was customary for me. I hated arriving late because when I was a boy Mom always arrived late with four kids in tow. Everyone always starred at me, and I hated it. Thus, being early eliminated that uncomfortable feeling.

I was standing in the rear of the sanctuary as guests were arriving. Al, my future father-in-law, was conversing with me as I greeted family and friends. I looked up to

Al and gave him my deepest respect. I never called him Dad; even though we had grown so close. I thought of him as a father but he never said anything about how he preferred to be addressed. It just felt right to call him Al and he didn't seem to mind. In the previous few months, he certainly showed me many aspects of being a good Dad. I admired his strength and boldness. His strong stature encouraged me to want to be like him. He gave me my first car, and I admired his generosity and kindness. I never had a male presence, other than my grandfather, give me so much confidence and courage. I listened to him, I loved him.

"This is your last chance, Jon," he blurted, as he chuckled under his breath. "There's the door. It's not too late!"

I just stood there with no reply. I thought this was odd coming from my future father-in-law. I thought, *Did he really want me to hurt his daughter? What was he saying? Did he know something? Did he sense what I had been trying to hide?* I chuckled with him and ignored what he said. I had no intention of running for the door. The thought of leaving Mona at the altar had never crossed my mind, and I certainly was not going to entertain the thought now. I dismissed the insurrection as nervous jesting.

Pastor Black was standing beside me behind the front altar. In a moment he would open that door and we would walk out in front of all my family, Mona's family, and our friends. This was my last moment before being legally bound to another person. My last moment of freedom. My last private selfish concern. Am I *ready for this?* I asked myself. *Will this fix me? Can I be true to her?* Doubt entered my mind for a second . . . then, another second. Time was approaching. Time. Pause. *This is right. Have confidence in your love.* I thought. Pastor Black opened the door.

Mona was so beautiful. Her gown was pure white. Lace, pearls, sparkles. She was so beautiful. My eyes fixated on hers as she walked down the aisle. She was clinging to her father's arm, and I noticed that he was almost in tears. I could feel my pantlegs shaking. *Were those my legs trembling?* Her gaze was straight forward on me, and the look in her eyes as she approached was unforgettable. She loved me. She wanted to be my wife. I took her hand. I claimed my vows.

I said, "I Do." Then, it was over. Quickly and nervously, I was married.

The nervousness didn't end with the ceremony. We soon left for our honeymoon. We stopped by Mona's parent's to pick up our luggage and change clothes. As we were leaving town, I fumbled with a can of cola I had grabbed to drink along the way and spilled it into my shoe. I was so nervous about what was to come. We arrived at our destination and checked into the hotel. Husband and wife—how strange. I carried my new bride across the threshold of the hotel room and placed her on the bed. We exchanged a kiss and gazed into each other's eyes.

It was late and the day had been so long. I suggested that we relax by taking a bath together. I went to the bathroom to fix my bride a nice soothing bathtub of warm water. I turned and found myself looking at my naked wife. I blushed. She slipped into the warm water and invited me to get undressed. I instantly became very self-conscious. I had never undressed in front of someone in the light before. I decided that it was now or never, then progressed to take off my clothes. My eyes were fixed on hers as I removed my under-shorts. She checked out all of me with her eyes scanning first down, stopping for a moment, then back up. I turned red, then joined her in the tub. I felt completely exposed inside and out. I had nothing to cover the shame I was feeling. I didn't know where it came from, but it was there. Inside. Deep inside. We finished relaxing in the tub, then went to bed. We turned out the lights, and I suddenly felt panic. *What do I do? How do I start? What do I do first?* I really didn't know what to do. I suddenly felt inadequate.

How can I share this vulnerability. I was a boy trying to be a man and failing at it miserably. I had no choice but to ask her to help me. I confessed my confusion, and she took the lead, placing my hand where she wanted it. I did what I thought she wanted and started kissing her neck. I fumbled to position myself above her. Awkward movements, strange fumbling. I was not good at this. She surely wanted something better than this. I had never done this before, and we were two virgins trying to act like we knew what we were doing. I certainly didn't, and I expected that instinct or mother nature would have kicked in gear by now. It wasn't happening. I tried to find her vaginal opening with my penis. Oh God, how awkward could this be. Where was it? I kept trying, until finally she grabbed my shaft and directed me to the right place. It didn't help. She was so dry it felt like sandpaper. *No! No! That couldn't be right.* I couldn't make penetration. Somebody just shoot me. Nobody told us about lubrication. Nobody gave me instructions or tips. *What the hell was I doing? Not having intercourse, that's what*! I finally gave up after Mona complained about being sore. I rolled over to my side in disgust; a tear slid to my pillow. Nobody could stand in this gap. Several days later I had the nightmare and struck the wall.

Chapter 8

Forgive Him

You, then, why do you judge your brother?
Or why do you look down on your brother?
For we will all stand before God's judgment seat.

Romans 14:10 (NIV)

Don't be left behind! *Behind what?* **You will surely perish!** *Why would I perish?* **Don't miss it!** *Miss what?* **Make your decision today!** *What do I need to make? Gosh, what was this guy talking about?*

Just months after our wedding, I was half listening to a television program, and some Evangelist was spouting off about accepting Christ as my Savior before it was too late. I didn't understand why it would be too late. I kept listening for the punch line. **Don't miss the Rapture!** *What is a rapture?* I asked myself. This didn't make any sense. I started listening, and then without pause, I understood what he meant.

I had always gone to church growing up but never had anyone explained to me what being "saved" was. Suddenly I understood. This guy wanted me to accept Christ into my heart, ask forgiveness for my sins and God would save me. *Save me from what?* **God will save you from yourself, your past, your sins, eternal damnation and God's judgment!** *Wow!, what a tall order. I thought* *it happened automatically from going to church all the time.* **God doesn't just hand it out without asking for His grace. You have to ask Him into your heart, then He will forgive every sin you've ever done!. You will be saved and raptured to be with Him forever. You will not be destroyed when Jesus returns to this earth!** *Wow, Jesus is going to destroy the earth? Man alive . . . . I need to be saved.* The man on TV prayed a simple prayer and I repeated after him. ***Jesus, please come into my heart and forgive me of my sins. I want to be with you in heaven. Please save me. Amen.***

Mona was in the next room. She had no idea I had just gotten saved! I didn't jump up and start shouting, my head didn't spin around three times nor did I even tell her what I had just decided. It was quiet, peaceful, personal, and uneventful.

Quiet, sometimes. Peaceful, assuredly. Personal, most definitely. Uneventful . . . absolutely not. In Psalm Chapter Two, David proclaimed a decree from the Lord and wrote, "You are my Son; today I have become your Father." You mean . . . *The Lord* just became my father? The Apostle Peter explains "In this you greatly rejoice, though now for a little while you may have had to suffer grief in all kinds of trials. These have come so that your faith—of greater worth than gold, which perishes even though refined by fire—may be proved genuine and may result in praise, glory and honor when Jesus Christ is reveled. Though you have not seen Him, you love Him; and even though you do not see Him now, you believe in Him, and are filled with an inexpressible and glorious joy, for you are receiving the goal of your faith, the salvation of your souls" (1 Peter 6-9 NIV). Uneventful? I don't think so. We read in Luke 15:10 (NIV), that Jesus said, *"In the same way, I tell you, there is rejoicing in the presence of the angels of God over one sinner who repents."*

Awesome! God is hearing rejoicing from the angels because of my decision.

The next day was Sunday. I told Mona that I wanted to go to church the next day. She didn't object. We woke early to arrive at church on time. We found a pew where we felt comfortable. So many new faces—some of whom came to greet us and welcome our presence. The service started and I could tell that Pastor Black spotted us in the crowd. After the service was over, he seemed to make a bee-line to us. He shook my hand and extended a warm welcome and asked us to return the next Sunday.

That next Sunday turned into many. We joined the evangelical church and became very involved in their ministry. Mona eventually accepted the Lord but really didn't get into the whole spiritual thing like I did. I was singing in the choir, teaching Sunday school, and helping with grounds maintenance. I enjoyed being a part of this family. It made me feel connected, and I liked most of the people I became acquainted with. Mona and I hadn't been married very long, and there were other couples there who were recently married also. Some became good friends, and we shared many personal outings and functions with several other couples our age.

My job during the early years of my marriage progressed and flourished. I was going to college for Industrial Technical Design at the local university. It was tough managing a career, obtaining a college education, and nurturing a family and church life, however Mona and I seemed to fit it all in and thrive while doing so. Work became an easy task. After a couple of years, drafting really didn't pose a challenge to me anymore. That was probably a good thing with all the other demands that we were facing. We purchased our first home during that first year and spent what spare time we had working on this one-hundred year old house. I enjoyed learning how to remodel by trial and error. Some things were a difficult challenge, but other tasks seemed to come second nature. I worked for a carpenter one summer during high school, building the house across the road from Mom and Dad's. So many of the skills I learned, now came in handy. I enjoyed owning a home. It was mine; I could do what I wanted with it, and it was big enough to start a family when the time came.

Only a few months had passed since I had the nightmare about Jett. I thought Mona had probably forgotten that night; she never brought it up. But I think she knew that it still haunted me. She knew that our home life was certainly not like my life with Jett, but I don't think she understood that those insecure feelings were still there. I didn't know what to do with them. When I dreamt about him, I just learned to not talk about it. I didn't want her to worry or think I would become violent; although, the dreams were always violent. I certainly didn't want another episode like before, or worse, so I decided that I would talk with Pastor Black to see if he had any advice.

I made an appointment, but I didn't tell Mona because I didn't want her to know the dreams were still occurring. I described to Pastor Black what the dreams were like and how they always ended in a physical confrontation. Sometimes they were very violent, and other times it was just an argument; however, they always woke me with great distress. My heart would be pounding in my chest and the adrenaline flowing through my veins with vengeance. And my behavior would become very aggressive when I felt threatened in any way. Sometimes I would snap at Mona for a simple infraction, which she not like or understand. She often commented that she felt like she was walking on eggshells around me—never knowing how I would react to any given situation. She could never discern if I would be mad and explode about something simple or just shut down emotionally. I asked Pastor Black what I could do to stop these dreams or change this behavior.

"You can't change it on your own Jon, but God can. You must forgive your brother for the past and leave it at the foot of the cross." he said.

"How?"

"We'll pray that God shows you how." he answered.

He prayed the most compassionate and empathetic prayer I had ever heard. He asked God to show me how to forgive Jett and leave the past behind. He stood in the gap for me before God. He asked for healing that I didn't know how to ask for or even thought I needed. He was wise and told me how to be effective in my prayers, not to be shy in asking God for his help.

Over the next several years, I spent many times in prayer at the altar asking for God's forgiveness and trying to forgive Jett.

In Ephesians Chapter 4, verse 32 (NIV), the apostle Paul writes, "Be kind and compassionate to one another, forgiving each other, just as in Christ, God forgave you." I understood what it said, but I didn't feel what it meant. My head knew what to do and what to say, but I didn't feel it in my heart. I couldn't get beyond the anger and hurt. How could I let that go? How could I just forget what he did to me and pardon his crimes? They were too great. They were too numerous. His actions violated the very heart of my existence. It was too humiliating and egregious to let go.

Eventually I started to question my approach to all of this. Maybe I wasn't making any progress because I was looking at it from the wrong direction. Then God showed me the deeper meaning of the latter part of that verse. *Through Christ, God forgave me.* Without Christ's suffering on the cross for my sins, I couldn't have been forgiven; and Christ died for everyone's sin, including Jett's, *including mine,* whether we know it or not. "For God so loved the world that He gave His one and only son, that whosoever believes in Him shall not perish but have eternal life" (John 3:16 NIV). Maybe this is what Pastor Black meant by "leaving it at the foot of the cross." In God's eyes my sin was just as ugly and egregious as Jett's. Romans 3:23 says, "For all have sinned and fall short of the glory of God." Who was I to think I was better than anybody else, including Jett. My sin was just as bad as his because we all sin. We can't escape it.

God was showing me I was accountable for not forgiving him. I didn't want to be accountable for this. I wanted it behind me. So I took all of the emotions, ill feelings, bad memories, anger, and deep hurt and said aloud in my soul, *Jesus, please take this. I can't carry it anymore.* At that moment I felt God's love envelope me with a warm and accepting, peaceful embrace. Warmth flowed over me, sweeping down my body. I bowed my face and closed my eyes when suddenly tears billowed, overflowing, gushing, streamed down my face into my mouth. I could taste the salt, purifying salt. I felt all of the heaviness leave my body as if it were pulled off me. I knew I had forgiven my brother. This process took seven years.

Chapter 9

It Shall Come To Pass

Behold, the former things are come to pass,
and new things do I declare:
before they spring forth I tell you of them.

Isaiah 42:9 (KJV)

I felt clean. A huge weight had been lifted from my soul. I thought I could almost fly if I wanted to. God was keeping His promises to me and demonstrating His faithfulness. I just had to trust Him. It didn't come easy; it took a lot of hard work, but I was determined to move forward. Trusting anything was certainly not in my comfort zone. And how could I trust something I couldn't see or touch. I could feel His touch upon me sometimes, but could I trust that it was God and not just some physiological kind of response to emotion? I just knew for sure that I didn't want to stay in that mire of bitterness. If this was the solution to that problem, I was willing to give it a try; I didn't have anything to lose except a bad attitude.

Everything started falling into place. Mona and I were happy. My job was secure, even though the economy in the early 80's was not. I was flourishing at church. I was elected a trustee at the church and was a member of the board. I was singing in a quartet, ministering at various churches in revivals. School was going well. Mona completed her education at Ohio State University and was making great strides in her career. I seemed to have time on my side. All of these responsibilities were keeping me busy, and I was content. My relationship with Mom and Dad was better. In fact, they started attending our church, even though they had to drive twenty-five miles one way. I guess time had a way of healing my mother's hurt caused by our marriage, and she really seemed to like Mona, once she allowed herself.

Our life fit into a neat little package with a pretty bow. The only thing missing was children. Mona and I talked about it several times over the past couple of years, but I wasn't sure I was ready for the responsibility of fatherhood. I thought that so many things were going well; why disrupt the apple cart?

I started doing a lot of traveling for my job. The economy was getting tight, so my boss decided that since there were little to no orders coming into the plant, the engineer that I worked under and myself could visit potential customers around the area to drum up some business. So, I started making sales calls to local factories offering our metal fabrication services. This went so well that the plant manager decided to expand our calling area to just about all of southern Ohio. This increased my driving to about five hundred miles per week.

I was driving south on one of the major interstate freeways, when I saw an adult bookstore advertisement on a billboard. It had a picture of a man and a woman on it. The man was so handsome, and he had his shirt off. He was just the type that I liked. I started thinking about him—not really him, but any man. Donny came to my mind. I could still smell his hair and taste his kiss. Memories of him caressing me suddenly made my pulse start racing. I was getting an erection while I was driving.

The exit approached, and I could see the sign for the bookstore. *Do I, or don't I?* I felt weak, as if in a daze but fully aware of what I was doing. I veered off the freeway and down the exit ramp. I turned and was soon parking my car. I sat there for a moment and contemplated whether I should go in or not. *How much cash did I have? Twenty-four dollars.* I looked at my gas gauge, and I had plenty of gas to get back home. I would have to skip lunch if I bought anything. I sat there and thought and thought some more. I had never been in one of these places. I wondered what they were like. I mustered up the courage to get out of my car and go in. I found a three-pack of gay porn magazines for eleven dollars. I couldn't help but regain my erection as I looked through the assortment of pornographic paraphernalia. I hustled to the front counter and quickly paid. I couldn't get out of there fast enough. My erection must have been noticed.

I felt like I had done something wrong, so I just started my car and left the parking lot as fast as I could. I was so ashamed of myself, that I drove down the highway for several miles before I realized I even had the magazines next to me. I took off the wrapper and gazed at the first cover. There was a naked man. At that point in my life, I don't believe I had ever seen full frontal male nudity, other than in the locker room at school, and even then I couldn't really look at anyone in fear of being ridiculed and humiliated. I quickly focused my vision back to my driving. I glanced over as I would turn a new page. How exhilarating! What was next? Oooh, he was good looking. Oh My! He was built. I couldn't wait to get home. I started driving faster and faster. If I hurried, I could get home before Mona by about an hour, and that would be enough time to satisfy myself. I was so excited. I kept stroking myself through my trousers, my pulse throbbing.

I felt guilty for pleasing myself. If Mona only knew I was fantasizing about men. I felt like I was betraying her. I hid the magazines where I knew she would never find them. I didn't want to throw them away, even though I felt ashamed of them. I couldn't let go of the lust; it felt so good. I just had to keep it a secret. I kept telling myself that she didn't have to know. This would be my secret, just for me. I didn't look at myself as being *gay. How could I?* I was married. I was just having a little bit of fun and it didn't have to involve her. But deep inside, I knew that getting married didn't fix me. It did nothing to rid me of the desires inside of me. *God, how was I going to control this? How could I keep this hidden?* I decided that I would just have to pray hard for God to remove it. He could do this for me; all I had to do was ask.

Dear Lord, I don't understand this.
I don't know why this is inside of me,
But I can't help it. I feel powerless to stop it.
Give me the strength to endure it.
Or you must take it from me.
In Jesus' name. Amen.

Many months went by as Mona and I talked about having a child. She expressed a lot of concern about being pregnant and giving birth. It was very scary to her. I really didn't understand her anxiety about the whole thing, but I tried. I rationalized her feelings by telling myself that women have babies every day and she would be fine, and soon she would be pregnant and not scared anymore. It was that simple. Her mother tried to reassure her that pregnancy was a blessed time, and that she would enjoy it.

We had been married six years, and we were both twenty-four years old. I was ready to be a father. I was anxious as Mona's fears finally gave way to consent. She made an appointment with her OB-Gyn and we started planning. Mona would have to be off her birth control pills three months before we could start trying. I could tell she was leery and full of fear, but she didn't change her mind.

My boss had just informed me that the company was up for sale. I was not happy. I worked for a family business and the founder of the company wanted to retire, but none of his sons were interested in continuing the task of managing the business. I knew that it was just a matter of time before everything changed. I could already feel the mood shift at work. It was time for me to move on. I hadn't completed my degree in engineering, but I soon had some leads that the local paper mill in the town where Mona and I lived might be interested in my talent. I had worked with one of their Engineers on several projects and he seemed to be impressed with my work. He soon arranged for me to have an interview with the Director of Engineering. I was hired that day and asked when I could start. I turned in my two week's notice even though I hated to. I didn't want to leave my first real job. I felt so comfortable and secure where I was, and I truly liked the people I worked for. Venturing into the unknown was terrifying for me.

I tried to look at the positive, being so close to home; I could literally walk to work everyday. But I was not embracing the change. It was a large corporation, in fact, the largest employer in three counties, with much better benefits, but I was still very insecure about the move. My pay increased about twenty-five percent, and I didn't have to drive twenty miles one way every day. I would be close when Mona delivered and when our child started school. I was hoping for better chances of advancement when I finished my degree; plus, they paid for most of my tuition. I was trying to convince myself that this was a good thing. I was planning for our future and hoping that I was making the right decision.

This probably wasn't very good timing, since I had just changed jobs, but we started planning the pregnancy as soon as three months were up. She was never comfortable with sex; I always blamed myself. But the more sex we had, the better I was with my other desires. Our sex life was never what I would call robust, but we eventually got the hang of it. Trying to get pregnant gave me a good excuse to get as much of it as I could. We met at home on our lunch hour for a nooner every day for about two weeks. The doctor advised us that mid-day was a woman's most fertile time of day. I surely didn't mind.

Mona missed her very first cycle period. We purchased a home pregnancy test even though it had only been two weeks. They were a fairly new thing—and not too reliable— but we couldn't wait to see what it told us. She used the test early in the morning on a Saturday. The instructions told her to urinate on the stick and wait twenty minutes. If she was pregnant, it would turn pink; if she wasn't, it would stay white. I couldn't wait any longer. I rushed into the bathroom after only fifteen minutes, I just had to see what it looked like. To my utter amazement, IT WAS PINK! We were pregnant! I was going to be a father! Wow!

I came running out of the bathroom waving the stick in the air. "We're pregnant! We're Pregnant!"

I immediately grabbed the phone and called her mom and dad. "We're pregnant! Mona's pregnant! We're going to have a baby!"

I didn't even give Mona a chance to respond. I think she was flabbergasted. I handed the phone to her as a tear came down her cheek. She talked to her mother for a short time and told her that we would be over to their house in a little while after we made more phone calls. She hung up and I immediately called my mother and father, then brothers and sisters. Everyone was greatly excited for us. I started writing letters to the baby.

Dear Baby,
I don't know what you are, but I know who you are.
You are my child. God is creating you from your mother
and me. I can't wait to see you, hold you, cuddle you,
smell you and of course love you. I am your father. I will
protect you and do my very best to raise you.
                                        Love, Dad

Chapter 10

The Stumble

They will not satisfy their hunger
or fill their stomachs with it,
for it has made them stumble into sin.

Ezekiel 7:19 (NIV)

Incredible! How incredible it was to hold my newborn son, Travis. I couldn't have been more proud or pleased. Mona was doing well, even though she had endured an exhausting delivery from twenty-two hours of labor and a cesarean section. I watched as she embraced motherhood with an amazing sense of nurturing. I had never witnessed this before. All at once I was filled with emotions. Vast, immense emotions. Holding him in my arms was real. It wasn't a vision, it wasn't my imagination, it was real. He was my flesh and blood, made in my image, made from me. What an awesome blessing God had given us. I recalled how excited I was when I was fifteen years old and had the vision of my son. I thanked God for His promise. God was faithful.

I was so excited everyday to quietly sneak into his nursery and watch him sleep. His little hands and feet, were so tiny and exquisitely made. Even his fingernails, were so perfect and minuscule. So pure and perfect. His innocence was overwhelming. His essence was so unadulterated. Without blemish, without any tainting. I didn't feel worthy to hold such a precious vessel in my arms—so opposite of what I had become.

My job had turned into a nightmare. I had taken a promotion into the Maintenance Department where I was responsible for all the planning and scheduling for a large production paper machine. It was extremely demanding as was my boss. To make matters worse, the production manager was an egocentric asshole who relished embarrassing and humiliating his staff. This made life unbearable for me. Working under these conditions stifled my ability to function at my best. Every decision, every effort was scrutinized and discredited. I found myself having anxiety issues. It digressed to the point that I didn't want to go to work any longer. I lay awake many nights listening to the sound of the plant, the constant humming and growling, like a living beast—just a few blocks away, permeating the still night air. I felt terror, knowing that my credibility and future were at stake. I decided to transfer back to the Engineering Department and swallow my pride. I felt like I had failed. After college, I decided to ask for an Associate Engineer's position. They granted my request but with an Project Engineer's position and assigned me to an older part of the plant with two smaller paper machines, because the engineer for that production area was being transferred. I was extremely blessed and relieved.

I learned a great deal about their production and maintenance. The largest of the two was scheduled for a complete rebuild and overhaul that next year. I was not only the project engineer for this task but also the coordinator with over fifty contractors, over one hundred maintenance staff and corporate personnel involved, along with production and scheduling staff, and I was only twenty-seven years old. It was an enormous and extremely demanding undertaking for which I had many self-doubts. This was do or die. The budget was twelve million dollars—the largest project I ever managed, and I was a green engineer.

Our successful completion was on time and under budget. I received many accolades and kudos along with another promotion. This was very beneficial to my career, as many corporate executives were looking at my management style. However, I became married to my job.

Our second child came into the world that next year. She was a precious little girl who looked just like her mother. Ashley had a cute button nose and lots of dark brown hair. She became the light of my life.

Ephesians 5:8-9 (NIV) says, "For you were once darkness, but now you are light in the Lord. Live as children of light (for the fruit of the light consists in all goodness, righteousness and truth)." For me this was a description of my inner secrets, exposing their darkness. I lived in darkness, hiding my deepest desires and fantasies. I couldn't bear the thought of exposing the secrets for fear of hurting everyone I loved. I didn't want to be responsible for destroying my precious children's home. I had no choice but continue keeping my private desires hidden, away from the light of day, away from my wife and family, away from my public life. How could I possibly be a good example to my children when I was living a lie, Providing it an outlet, just by myself, seemed perverse and twisted, but what choice did I have? I couldn't stop it. I couldn't share it. I couldn't confess it. I couldn't even live with it. I started hating myself for not being able to get rid of it. I couldn't expose the truth. *How could the Lord understand this? How could he forgive me?* It didn't make sense to me, even though I kept praying for God to remove it or fix it. How could I live in goodness and righteousness? *God, are you hearing my prayers?*

I wanted to be a light to my children, but as Ashley grew, I couldn't help but know that my inner desires were growing. I started to realize that having children did not fill that hole I felt in my heart. I hated to think that I couldn't fix the problem; after all, I was a problem solver by nature and education. It seemed that the more responsibilities I had, the more pressure and tense my life had became. Sometimes when I was alone with the two children, the chaos and heaviness of the responsibility seemed too much. I really started to doubt my ability to be a good father. It was sometimes difficult to focus on their needs.

I started noticing that my mind would drift away and daydream about being with a man. I realized when I passed a couple on the street, I would look at the man and not the woman. I would gaze at his crotch and try not to be obvious. Trying to understand why this had become so consuming was robbing me of my peace.

The financial controller had informed my boss that he was interested in creating a new position for the Engineering Department focusing on cost management. My boss explained what the parameters would be and asked if I could put some ideas down on paper. Over the next two weeks I developed a comprehensive plan outlining the variables and constraints involved with project management within the system structure at the plant. I reviewed every aspect of an Engineer's task concerning spending management focusing on the time required to do so and how this was affecting an engineer's effectiveness. I submitted it to my boss and the CFO. They both raved about how it could impact our department. Within a week, I was offered the management position of

Cost Control Administrator; I accepted without hesitation. I was extremely excited about this new endeavor.

I spent the next several months developing financial policies and procedures while implementing new directives. The department purchased a computer for the task of cost tracking, and I quickly learned how to operate and manage software. I also immediately endeavored to develop software using techniques I learned managing my own projects. Coming from an engineer's perspective, knowing what was helpful in project management, I was able to capture real time costs as they occurred within any given project. This gave the engineers a tool to use in keeping control of their spending. This greatly reduced cost overruns and over committing available capital. The CFO became my biggest fan, sometimes stepping on toes to make policy and procedure work for this new control system. The President and CEO of this worldwide company even came and spent an afternoon with me to see how my system worked. However, I was not everybody's best friend. It wasn't long before several nicknames became common when referring to me. I didn't care; I knew my job, and I did it well. I learned that making enemies didn't serve me very well, especially when a stumble turns into a fall.

I arrived home from work at my usual time. Mona was at home, which was a normal schedule for her to have a mid-week day off. I bounded up the stairs to find her in our bedroom cleaning. As I entered the room, she turned toward me holding my porn magazines.

"What are these?" she demanded!

I turned and walked out of the room dumbfounded. I didn't know what to say, so I turned and left, pretending I didn't even hear her. *How did she find them? How can I face this? I'm not prepared for this. Did she have suspicion and went looking for them?* I couldn't process what just happened. I could only imagine what she was thinking. *Oh God! This is awful. What was I going to tell her?*

She came downstairs, and we prepared dinner. The children were playing in the living room. The silence between us was deafening. The whole time my mind was racing, unfocused, and mechanical. She must hate me. What was she thinking? Not a word. Not a word.

The rest of the evening we sat in front of the television in a daze. The kids played in the middle of the room, and we both tried to ignore the elephant sitting there too. It was unbearable. It came time for Travis and Ashley to go to bed, and my heart sank into my stomach. *How was I going to explain this? How could I help her understand? God, please give me the words.*

I came down the stairs and sat down on the sofa. I could see her descend the stairs with a grimaced look on her face. By the time she entered the living room, she was in full tears. The heartbreak was evident and swift.

"Can you explain why you had those magazines?" she asked.

"No, I really can't," I replied.

"Why in the hell do you have those magazines?" she demanded. "Are you gay?"

"No . . . . I don't think so."

"What do you mean, you don't think so? Have you been with someone?"

"No, I haven't been with anyone, not since we've been engaged to be married."

"So, you have been with a man before?" she continued to question me like an interrogator.

"Yes, a long time ago," I replied.

"So, you are gay! Why in the hell did you marry me? Our whole marriage has been a lie! Why didn't you tell me?" she projected.

"I didn't know myself. I thought getting married would fix this. I swear, Mona, I haven't been with anyone. I've been faithful to you, but I've had this inside me and kept praying that God would take it from me or fix me somehow, but He hasn't. I swear! I didn't know what to do about it," I cried as I tried to explain.

"When did you buy the magazines?" she asked.

"A long time ago when I was traveling making sales calls."

"That long ago?" she protested. "And you've never confided in me all of this time?"

"No, I didn't know how. I didn't want to hurt you. You must believe me," I pleaded.

"I don't know what to believe anymore. Have you touched Travis?" she asked.

"Absolutely not! How could you think such a thing? He's my son for God's sake!"

"Leave God out of this. Don't blame Him!" she protested.

We spent three hours crying, talking, explaining, screaming, and crying some more. I vowed that I would not act upon my homosexual feelings without telling her. I felt that I owed her, and she vowed to increase our intimacy. I explained to her that whenever there was a long pause between out times of intimacy, the feelings became stronger. At this point we had been married for twelve years, so our sexual episodes were sometimes two months apart. I also explained that it made me feel neglected when she wouldn't return my affections. I didn't blame her, but I wanted her to understand what I was experiencing. We went to bed exhausted.

The next day I felt absolutely free. It felt like the entire world had been lifted off my shoulders, and I didn't have to hide anymore. Of course, the reality was that I did have to hide at my job and at church, but I didn't have to pretend with her. I could tell that she was not comfortable with this new revelation, but I hoped in time she would come to understand what I was dealing with all of these years. I'm sure she would have rather ignored the problem or pretended it didn't exist, but I could tell that there was no denial every time she looked at me. I knew it was painful for her. I knew it hurt her. I knew that she was questioning all of our past and the love that we shared, but at least she knew the truth now. At least she knew the real me. I didn't have anything to hide now.

This gave me a new reality, a new freedom. I felt empowered to explore "me". My personality started to change. I was more outgoing, and energetic. I started to explore myself sexually. I began to manipulate my personal satisfaction with more anal stimulation. I began to discover about myself what really pleased me sexually. I was never with another man, but my fantasies became more involved. I wasn't embarrassed, nor did I feel bad or guilty for expressing myself. It gave me great pleasure and acceptance for who "I" was. It didn't matter any more that she didn't show any interest in me. I didn't feel ashamed or rejected any more. I started to actually feel normal, more of a man, more complete. I may have been in denial that my marriage was falling apart, but I felt more together than I ever had in the past.

Chapter 11

The Fall

You have set our iniquities before you,
our secret sins in the light
of your presence.

Psalm 90:8 (NIV)

I entered the dark room. The lighting was dim and foreboding, preventing me from seeing everyone in the bar. It was a small establishment with barely room for thirty people, although recently built; it was very accommodating for meeting people on the down low. I found a bar stool at the very end of the counter, so I could survey the clientele easily as they came to the bar to order drinks. Not really my cup of tea, so to speak, but it would do.

I heard of this new bar when it had its grand opening several months before. It was a big topic of conversation at work because it was a "gay" bar, and everyone was making fun of it. One of the engineers I worked with was a republican city councilman, and he had received an invitation to their opening celebration. He showed it around the office cracking jokes about the "faggots" that would be there.

The music was loud, forcing me to talk louder than usual to order a simple drink. A tall Bacardi and Coke was my preference, and I watched the bartender fix the drink as I casually observed people mingle. I wasn't a big socializer, in fact, a bit dysfunctional when I was out of my comfort zone, which certainly described my insecurity. I noticed a certain group of younger males conversing and carrying on, seemingly celebrating some occasion. They would order quite a slammers for just the few at their table. I continued looking and watching them from a distance, trying not to be obvious. I noticed that one of them glanced in my direction a few times, which eventually gave me the opportunity to make eye contact with him.

He was attractive, much younger than I, stout with dark hair. He was wearing tight jeans and a dress shirt, neatly pressed. He walked with a bit of a slide to one side. He was cute. He kept my interest for the next hour, as I continued to order my cocktail of choice. I wondered if I dare talk to him. Would he reject me? After all I was older and not as attractive as he was, at least by my perception. Every once in a while he would glance over at me, and I decided that in and of itself was enough cue for me to make an approach. I did, and we started chatting. Bryce was an assistant manager at one of the local banks, single, and very much interested in me. I asked if he would be interested in blowing off this joint and coming over to my place for some privacy. (What a line. Ha!) We were soon driving out of the parking lot. We pulled into my driveway and I motioned for him to park in the spare spot in the garage.

We were soon enthralled in a very intimate embrace in the living room. I could feel his erection through his pants. My pulse was racing. I invited him upstairs to my bedroom, and he obliged. He stripped in front of me with no compunction. I couldn't believe how comfortable he was with his nudity. I was very excited. I reciprocated, removed my underwear and although I was confident with my body, I felt embarrassed by his staring. The next thing I knew, he knelt in front of me.

Earlier That Day

My wife was out of town at a Karate' tournament with Travis. I was required to work because one of my machines was shutdown for repairs. I called repeatedly to their hotel room with no answer. Finally, late that afternoon, Travis answered the phone.

"Hey sport . . . . how's the tournament going?"

"Ok, I guess," Travis replied.

"Where's mom?"

"She's downstairs watching Mick fight."

"Who's with you?" I inquired.

"Sherrie. We're having pizza," he answered.

"Okay bud, have a good time. I'll see you tomorrow. I love you."

"I love you too Dad. Bye."

I hung up the phone and stared out the kitchen window. My thoughts went back in time when all of us would watch Travis perform at his karate' lessons. We urged him on and encouraged his interest. Little did I know that my wife had an interest in someone other than her son. I kept asking myself, *Why would she watch Mick fight?* I had my suspicions about him in the past, and I didn't trust him. I guess it was the way he always talked to Mona at the dojo. He had an extremely large ego, certainly not afraid to talk to a married woman, even when her husband was around. This sent many red flags up the pole for me, and when I expressed them to Mona, she always told me that I was overreacting.

Then I noticed that she started fixing herself up a bit more than usual to take Travis to his karate' practices. Mona had an unconscious way of applying too much makeup, which I noticed time and time again. I suddenly remembered all of these actions and I got a sinking feeling in my stomach. *What's good for the goose is good for the gander* was my thinking. That was when I decided to check out the new bar in town. I made arrangements for Ashley to spend the night at her aunt's.

I was whole. I was satisfied. I was elated. My emotions were soaring to a height I had never felt before. My body was literally tingling all over. My mind was racing with ecstasy as I pondered the previous three hours with Bryce. Every sense was heightened, every emotion exhilarated. On one hand I had just committed adultery, and on the other, I experienced sexual perfection, which I had not experienced since I was a teenager. My soul felt like it was ablaze with passion. I had denied myself this passage for so many years, thinking that it could be fixed or nullified. It never was. The Lord never removed it, covered it, or bore it for me. It was never denied to me, but I denied it. This experience unlocked who I really was. I felt a sense of completeness like I never had before. I felt strong, confident, and virile. I thought of Donny even though it was fifteen years earlier. It couldn't be hidden or denied any longer. My spirit was soaring, and I couldn't hide that either.

It was Memorial Day weekend. Mona was in Cleveland, and we were to meet at my parents home on Monday to celebrate the holiday with my family. I brought Ashley with me to the farm, and soon Mona arrived with Travis. The greeting seemed trite. I know I was distant, but so was Mona. We spent the day with the family as usual, trying to ignore the mundane and pretend we were enjoying ourselves. Mona and I both knew that something was different, but we kept our thoughts to ourselves. We returned home that evening, put the children to bed, and retired to television and silent conversation.

The next day I went about my normal routine, went to work, and had a normal day. It would be the last one. Late in the afternoon I contacted Mona's sister and asked if she could care for the children that evening because Mona and I had a serious situation to deal with. She tried to inquire for more information, and I told her that I would give her an explanation when I arrived. She agreed. I picked up the kids from the babysitter's and headed to my sister-in-law's home. The kids loved their aunt's house, so they immediately ran upstairs to play. They had no idea that their world was about to explode. And all the while, deep inside of me, I felt a strong peace or assurance that I was doing the right thing. Patty started asking me many questions; I stopped her and simply said, "I'm gay". Her verbal tracks stopped cold with a blank stare, then she slowly closed her mouth.

"Mona or I will call later." as I bounded to the car. I drove off, never looking back, never searching for a reaction.

Next, I drove to my mother and father-in-law's house. When I entered the back door, Al was sitting at the kitchen table as he often did. He gleefully asked if I wanted a cup of coffee, which I declined.

"I have some news that you both need to hear," I announced.

I moved to the living room where Alice was sitting and I could tell that Al was behind me. I closed my eyes and said, "Mona is going to need a shoulder to cry on tonight. I'm gay."

The room was silent.
Still and silent.

"I will be telling her when she gets home from work tonight, but I wanted you to know first." I was blubbering, and could hardly finish the sentence.

With my head hung and tears falling to the carpet, Al put his arm around my shoulders and through his tears he said, "We're so sorry, Jon."

I turned and left as quickly as I could, knowing I had just broken the hearts of the two dearest people I had ever known. I watched the tears fall to the concrete as I passed through the garage, and even though I knew that I had done the right thing by telling them, I couldn't help but feel like my honesty was worth nothing. My heart was breaking. I felt hollow and brittle. I had laid everything bare for everyone to see, and I was not proud. But the hardest was yet to come and I knew it.

When I arrived home, the house was empty. I looked around and sensed a stinging in my heart. I knew what I was about to tell Mona was going to absolutely rip her world apart. I knew she trusted me. I knew she was depending on me to lead an upright life of honesty and integrity. *Was I destroying that? Was I betraying that trust, or was I honoring that promise I had made to her? How could doing the right thing be so painful and cause so much hurt and destruction?* Yet at the same time, I was free. I was absolutely elated to know that I needed to be with a man to be complete and happy. I was actually relieved to have finally been with a man, in an adult sense, as a man. *God what have I done? God, where are you? Has what I've done caused God to abandoned me?*

*For the Lord your God is a merciful God;
He will not abandon or destroy you or*

Forget the covenant with your forefathers,
Which He confirmed to them by oath.

Deuteronomy 4:31 (NIV)

Had God abandoned me? Did my sin of adultery separate me from my God? How do I search for these answers when so much of the world has told me I am wrong for being this way? How do I find God's heart and find out how He feels about this? Was I supposed to just give up on my marriage? So many questions and not enough answers.

Mona locked eyes with me as she entered the adjacent room and didn't move them or blink as she approached me. As I sat on the sofa watching her get closer, I could tell by her expression that she knew something was wrong. Although there was a lot wrong with our marriage, we were very in tune with each other as close friends. We could tell what each other was thinking at times, and finish each other's sentences most of the time. We shared many intimate details and thoughts with each other through the years, but I was sure she couldn't read my mind this time.

I invited her to sit on the sofa beside me as I reached for her hand. I tried to brace her for the bad news by prefacing that I had already spoken to her mother and father, and they already knew what I was about to tell her. I didn't know how else to say it, but to, just say it. I told her I met a man over the weekend and we had been intimate. She asked "how intimate," and I explained the details to her. Through rain-drop tears, she expressed her grief, her damnation, her betrayal, her sorrow. I was surprised that she didn't yell, throw anything, or hit me; as I had imagined that she would. She handled her composure as best as anybody possibly could; then, she asked me to leave. I hurriedly grabbed a few things and left. I drove to the farm as quickly as I could because I felt myself falling apart.

I arrived at my parent's house completely and absolutely devastated by what I had just done. I knew it was right to tell her the truth, but I hated the consequences. I felt naïve, stupid, and puerile. I entered the front door, and Mom immediately asked what had happened. I just started spewing out all of these details, of which they had no clue. It was completely unexpected and raw to them. My father sat in the chair across from me completely silent. His hand perched on his cheek like it had been glued there. My mother gasped while trying to understand the severity of the situation with a thousand impromptu questions. I realized I had just turned everyone's world upside down. I was numb. I needed a reassuring hug, an encouraging word. I went to bed alone for the first time in fourteen years, with neither.

Chapter 12

Where Do I Go From Here?

Search me, O God,
And know my heart; try me,
And know my thoughts.

Psalm 139:23 (KJV)

search \ 'serch \ *vb:* to make painstaking
investigation or examination.
(Websters Ninth New Collegiate Dictionary)

I began searching for my justification. How could I be a Christian *and* be gay? The pain of what Mona and I were experiencing was too great to focus on or even think about. I needed to find a way to understand what was happening in my life. I needed to reconcile my desire for men and my love for the Lord. But how? Nobody in the church could help me. I couldn't confide in my pastor about what we were going through. Instinct told me that, not only was it unacceptable, but I would be harshly scrutinized and ridiculed. This was a private matter, and Mona and I would deal with it as such.

I decided to seek the help of a counselor who was contracted through a help center at work. The meeting would be confidential, and nobody needed to know what we were discussing. I made an appointment and was able to meet with Carolyn that afternoon. She was very warm and reassuring, as she explained to me that the sessions were completely confidential. The only reporting she was required to do was just by number of clients only. I felt confident and safe to discuss my situation with her. I spilled my guts, and I do mean everything. I told her that I wasn't sure what effect this was going to have on my marriage; Mona may want to divorce me. My family was not reacting well to the news. And I didn't know how to relate to this new self-revelation, given the fact that I was a devout Christian. She really had no answers for me, but gave me some direction on where to start my search to reconcile my faith.

I made a visit to the library and performed a catalog search using "gay" to see what showed up; mostly trash. I performed another catalog search using "Christian" and found a plethora of references. I painstakingly went through each one and happened across three different publications concerning Christianity and Homosexuality. This was 1992, so there wasn't much to go on. I found them and signed them out. Two books were in support of my situation, and one told me I would go to hell. I really don't remember their titles, but I do remember one was written by a Catholic priest. I eagerly delved into the publication hoping to find some kind of epiphany. It never came, but it did help me understand human sexuality in a way that I never had before. And, because of that, I hesitated in blaming myself for the way God made me. After all, I didn't create my own internal wiring in my brain. I knew I didn't choose to be this way.

I returned home that next day to find Mona cold and unresponsive. I couldn't blame her. I actually understood where she was coming from. But even with that, it didn't curtail my inner exhilaration and peace with the truth. I couldn't apologize to her for it, although, I did for the infidelity. It was hard to separate the two, especially with her interpretation of the event. She was so angry. Angry at me, angry at what I had done. She blamed herself for not seeing the truth, and for trusting me to keep it under control, or not acting on it. She didn't understand I was on a journey of discovery that couldn't be stopped. The gate was open, and I walked through it. Her discovery of the magazines only made it easier for me to embrace that discovery and feel the empowerment of it. I couldn't apologize for who I was. I had to be true to myself. The only question left was, did she want to remain married?

I gave her a couple of days to ponder our predicament; during which time I hardly communicated with her at all. I gave her all the space she needed, and I slept in Travis' room while we tried to figure out our future. We went about our routines, going through the motions without arguments or discussions. Then, after several days had passed, I asked her if she wanted a divorce. She answered me with a question, "Are you still going to be gay?" This told me she obviously didn't understand. She must have thought this was something I could change. I explained to her that this was who I was, and it wasn't going to change. I couldn't go backwards in my self-discovery. I tried to explain to her I still loved her, I still valued our marriage, but I had changed. I would no longer live with this denial, trying to cover up who I really was. At the same time I truly loved my wife. I didn't want to give her up, but I also realized that I most likely couldn't have both. I knew that it would lead to a sacrifice on both our parts that would truly be extremely painful for both of us. I felt I had to make an undeniable decision because I could no longer offer her the future that she deserved. She deserved to have a faithful husband with whom she could be intimate and have a satisfying sexual relationship with. I didn't feel that I could provide that any longer. I was no longer the husband that she needed.

Nothing or no one could possibly fill this gap. The expanse was wide and growing wider. I removed my wedding ring, knowing I could no longer perform my duty or responsibility as a husband. The void was deep, sudden, and final. There was no possibility of a bridge and nothing could fill in the gap. Everything I had known for the past fourteen years was suddenly coming to an end, and all I could think of were my selfish needs. I was paralyzed to even think of telling the children that I was leaving. I couldn't bear the thought of not seeing them every day, yet I knew that it was a real possibility in the near future. My heart was broken, and I could only imagine what Mona was feeling. I thought that the best thing to do was to let her make the emotional break and not even ask her about her feelings.

She needed to shift her focus away from me and onto survival. Survival of her and the children on their own without me. I knew there was no asking for shared parenting; it was completely out of the question for her. I figured I would just have to give her whatever she wanted in a settlement since I was the one who broke the vows and violated our covenant. The penalty would be steep, but what choice did I have? I couldn't fight her on it; I couldn't even fight for myself. I just knew I needed to be on my own to discover who I was and what I wanted.

I had just arrived home from work, and the phone rang. It was Pastor Black. A week had passed since my revelation to Mona, and I immediately wondered if he knew. He cut right to the chase and answered my question rather quickly.

"I understand you're gay!" he said abruptly. "Do you intend on living a "gay" lifestyle?"

I replied, "Well I guess so, whatever you think that means."

"In that case, I must inform you that we have revoked your membership with the denomination and ask you return any keys that you might have for the church."

"If that is what you want, I will do that, but first, don't you care that I still love God and I need my church family right now? I could really use some guidance and support from my spiritual family, and Mona and I are in great pain from this. Is that important to you at all?"

"We would be glad to minister to any of Mona's needs if she desires. Please leave your keys with the church secretary."

Click!

I stood there gazing out the kitchen window with the phone receiver in my hand. I was stunned. I couldn't believe what I just heard. The gap just widened.

Now what? What do I do? Where do I go from here? God, what am I supposed to do now? I've destroyed my I've alienated my church. All this, and for what? To be true to myself? To be who I really am? At what cost and to whom? Is this really worth it? Is it the path I'm supposed to take? If it is, then I have really made a mess of it. Why is this so painful? Why am I alone? Where are you? Do you care?

I began to cry in despair. The reality of my decision was hitting me hard in my gut. It felt as if a two-ton safe had just dropped on my head. I realized I was alone and processing this drastic change by myself. I had nobody to lean on or talk to who had been through anything like this. Nobody to give me advice. *Where do I go from here?*

I called my folks every day on my lunch hour. For the first few days, Dad would answer the phone, then suddenly hand it to Mom without a word. After a day or two, he stopped answering. If Mom was available when I called, she would answer, and I would hear him leave the room or go outside. He didn't even want to know I was calling.

Then, eventually she told me that he didn't want to ever see me again. He not only wouldn't talk to me, he was turning his back on me. I needed him. I needed a strong man to help guide me through this emotional nightmare. But what was I to expect? He had never been there for me growing up. Why should this be any different? I couldn't have been more isolated. My only ray of hope was my mother. She told me several times she didn't understand. She said I couldn't expect her to change the way she was brought up and change the way she had been thinking for sixty years. To her, it was a sin. No question, no debate, no possible refute from God. It was final. Sin! Unforgivable, abominable sin! Punishable by death and certain condemnation to hell. Repent, Repent, Repent, or perish.

I pondered in my heart what to say to her. *Wait! God made me this way. I didn't choose it. I've begged God to get rid of it, to take it from me. He didn't do it. And I asked thousands of times. I was on my face in prayer, begging for Him to remove it from me. He didn't. I've cried, pleaded, and begged for Him to take this from me, and He wouldn't do it. How could I possibly choose this. How could I go against a God whom I had served, and loved, and cherished so very much. You've got to believe me, this is His plan for my life. I don't understand why, and I don't know how I will make it through this. But I will. I need your love and I need your help. Please!*

The silent conversation quickly ended.

"We'll talk again tomorrow. I love you. Bye," was all she said.

A couple of days went by, and I received a phone call from Pastor Black. He stated that he would like to meet with me for a closed-door meeting. I agreed.

When I arrived, he kindly invited me into his office. I sat in a chair opposite his desk; then, he picked up the phone and quietly said, "He's here." I must have had a puzzled look on my face, when the associate pastor arrived and took a seat in the chair next to me. Pastor Black initiated the conversation by stating what he understood about me and Mona's situation.

"So, Is it true that you want to live the homosexual lifestyle?" he asked.

"I suppose that's true, now that these feelings have been exposed for the world to see. What choice do I have? The damage has been done." I replied.

The associate pastor asked, "Have you been with a man?"

"Yes," I answered.

"What did you do sexually?" He interrogated.

I turned to face him, "Well, I really don't believe that is any of your concern, with all due respect, of course."

"Mr. Lewis, we must be able to determine if you committed adultery so we know how to proceed with your case."

"Why, so you can lambaste me and crucify my actions?" I angrily stated. "Please . . . ."

Pastor Black interrupted, "Jon, did you have sex with a man?"

By this time I realized this was a witch-hunt and I was not going to survive the inquisition, so I replied with intent dismay, while staring straight into his eyes, "It depends on your definition of sex."

"Did you have any sexual contact?" he replied.

I answered with a direct and dissuaded tone, "I don't think this witch hunt is going to benefit anybody. Furthermore, I don't appreciate the tone of voice that has been used so far in this investigation."

As I rose to turn and leave, I added, "This conversation is over, gentlemen, and quite frankly, I don't care what you decide to do."

I returned to my car in tears. *God, Where do I go from here?*

Chapter 13

The Romans

*He is despised and rejected of men; A man of sorrows,
and acquainted with grief: and we hid as it were
our faces from him; he was despised and we
esteemed him not.*

Isaiah 53:3 (KJV)

I was facing many reconciliations: with my father, with my faith, with my church, with my wife, and one I was completely unaware of.

A couple of weeks had passed since that Memorial weekend, and although things were falling apart at home, I found solace throwing myself into my work. It was very task-oriented, and that alone provided me with the perfect distraction from everything racing through my soul. My brain could operate on auto pilot—at least for the time being—while Mona and I sorted this out.

It was a Friday afternoon, late in the work day, and fellow employees were starting to filter out of the department. This was when I usually did the week's filing and organizing for the following weeks tasks. A fellow engineer walked by my office and noticed I was still there. He was the former councilman who I mentioned earlier. He stopped at my door, and we started chatting cordially. I noticed that he seemed a bit more arrogant than usual, but I didn't give it a second thought until he asked about my divorce. I informed him my wife and I were not divorcing, but I was curious what he had been told. His reply shocked me.

"Well, I was told that you're a queer and your wife is leaving you."

I replied, "And you know this, how?"

"Everybody knows it," then he walked off.

I guess I shouldn't have been shocked because we did live in a small town. I knew Mona had confided in a few friends, and of course, I knew the church knew. I wondered if rumors really spread that quickly? Did people really gossip? What is wrong with these people? This is 1992. Gay people are in every facet of life. What was the big deal?

I suddenly felt exposed and naked. I knew the people I worked with and realized they could be very vicious and deceptive. I couldn't help but wonder who actually knew, and what had they been told. I wondered if my boss would exact any kind of punishment upon me; after all, he was a retired Navy Commander. I could only imagine what he thought of gay people, much less, what my co-workers thought. I was convinced the only way through this was to be confident, professional, and somewhat delusional in convincing myself that everything was okay. How could everything fall apart so quickly?

The rumors started flying around the office, and simple everyday tasks of just helping others in a daily course of work became excruciating. Staff meetings became humiliating and degrading at best. Comments were made, "I don't want to sit beside him; I might get Aids." I even became the butt-end of a few jokes floating around the office. It was becoming abundantly clear that

I was the talk of the town. Some would snicker when I walked by, and some would just shake their heads. Some of the engineers I worked with were genuinely nice, but others in the office were vicious and loved to gossip. My job became increasingly difficult to deal with, but I was focused on my work with an increasingly bitter attitude.

I was suddenly faced with so many issues I had not thought of. I couldn't help but wonder how this was going to affect my appraisal and my good standing; although, in my opinion, it shouldn't matter. *How do I reconcile what I feel in my heart and how everyone is treating me? How do I have faith through this time when everyone is turning their back on me?*

Travis and Ashley! They weren't turning their back on me. In fact, it seemed as if they needed me more. Maybe they could sense that something was drastically wrong at home. The guilt was piling up and consuming my subconscious. I could feel it, and it wasn't pleasant. *What do I do with all of this guilt and shame?* Some of it seemed natural, but most of it was accumulating from weeks of forced demoralization. The task of going to work everyday and performing such exacting and deliberate deeds for people who obviously felt repulsed and threatened by my identity, was becoming more than I could stand. My life-force was tired and becoming weak. I felt very vulnerable and inadequate but most of all a target.

I decided that the situation required me to move out of the house. Mona was not giving me an answer concerning a divorce. I was beating a dead horse staying there trying to make things work. My emotions were on auto pilot, and I knew I had to tell the children I was leaving. My heart was so heavy, finally reaching the point of running from the pain. I had to leave, but what was this going to do to them?

Knowing that I was going to break their hearts was breaking mine. Mona agreed that we should sit them down and tell them of my plans. Travis sat on the sofa across the room from me, and Ashley was sitting beside me. Daddy's little girl was never far from my lap. They knew that mommy and daddy weren't getting along, but they had no idea of the bomb I was about to drop. *How can I hurt them?*, I kept thinking. I had no choice. We started explaining what was happening but it seemed so inadequate. Then the moment came."

"Daddy is moving out," I blurted.

A look of such deep despair came over Travis as a tear hit the floor. His countenance plummeted into a desperate display of pain, as his eyes stared at me as if to look through my soul. Then Ashley started crying as if prompted from her brother. They were crushed.

"Will we ever see you again?" he asked brokenly through his tears.

"Yes, son. Of course. I'll still see you everyday. Daddy has an apartment just a few blocks away, and you can even help me pack and box things up. Daddy loves you very much, and you'll see that everything is going to be fine."

Mona stayed silent as she consoled Ashley. Travis started cheering up a bit when I told him he could dumpster dive for boxes for me. He crawled off the couch and gave me a big hug.

"I love you, Daddy," he said as he dried his tears and cuddled in my arms.

"I love you too, Kiddo." I replied, cherishing the moment with pain and relief. I looked at him intently wondering if damage had been done, knowing this moment would be one he would remember all of his life. I looked to Ashley, only just turning four and wondered if she understood I wouldn't be here anymore. Would she remember later in life?

Fireworks! The upcoming weekend was the Fourth of July. I had moved out of my house and decided that I would give the house to Mona and the kids. I was living in a duplex on Second Street, just a few blocks from the kids. Dad was still not speaking to me and barely anyone else. Out of the blue, Ellen called me and invited me to the "Red White and Boom" celebration in downtown Columbus. She worked downtown for a large corporation, and they allowed employees and their families to view the fireworks from their roof and parking garage.

"Mom and Dad are going to be there, aren't they?" I asked.

She replied, "Yes."

"But Dad doesn't want to see me!"

"He'll just have to get over that!" she stated with no uncertainty.

"Okay where and when?"

I decided to go last minute. The traffic was unbearable. I had to walk two miles just to get downtown where I was to meet my family. I wondered how I was ever going to find them, and when I did, how would they react? Probably not a smart idea to do this in public, but nonetheless, I trusted Ellen.

I arrived to our meeting spot right on time. After just walking two miles and up four flights of parking garage stairs, a big sigh exhaled from my mouth. My eyes started scanning all the people gathered for the show. Vendors were selling their hot dogs and drinks. People were hustling by. Loud talking and music filled the atmosphere. Suddenly I spotted Dad. He was walking crossways in front of me. I started toward him, knowing that he had not spotted me yet. I had a large lump in my throat, anticipating what would happen next. He turned his head toward me and caught my gaze. He instantly changed his gate and began walking straight for me. I tried to have a smile, but wasn't sure if it was manifesting on my face or not. As Dad approached me, I extended my hand to greet him with a handshake. He ignored it as if it weren't there and reached his arms around me and pulled me into a hug. A real, honest, vulnerable hug. I was stunned. I was relieved.

"Are you all right with this?" I asked.

He answered, "Sure."

No other discussion was needed. He escorted me to the place where the family had settled to watch the fireworks. Ellen hugged me and gave me a smile as if she knew everything was okay now, and the rest of the evening was quite perfect.

However my existence was far from perfect in this small town. I was beginning to wonder if my life would ever be normal again. I was continuing to go to church even though many people made it very clear I was not welcome. People I had known for years, that I thought would be understanding, were ostracizing me. I just kept thinking I was the same person I had always been, they just didn't know my secret.

I still cared about these people. I even truly loved some, but love was no longer being returned. I knew God loved me and that should be enough, but the gap in my faith was growing bigger. The gap at work was gasping wide open also. *How could I continue holding on to both sides of these gaps? Who would understand and show some compassion?* It felt like everybody had abandoned me. I was alone, isolated, and thrown away. Nobody wanted to console me. Nobody wanted to even talk to me. My pristine reputation was destroyed. I used to be the golden boy; now, I was nothing but trash everyone seemed to want to throw away.

My new apartment became my refuge. I could shut the world away and deny what was happening by drowning myself in my music. I listened to all of my old albums over and over again, looking for some solace. To no avail, depression was starting to command my thoughts. Going to bed was the only relief I could find. I wasn't in pain when I was sleeping, so it became my relief. However, this relief that was shattered one evening after going to bed.

I had just slipped under my safe, warm covers, trying to release the concerns of the divorce, the trials of the day, and the uncertainty of the future. Praying didn't seem to work, only sleep. Then the phone rang. I answered.

"I know who you are, and I'm going to take care of you!" said a strange voice.

"What? Who is this?" I quickly replied.

No answer. Silence. Click!

I immediately called the police. The dispatcher connected me to the detective on duty. I informed him of the phone call I had just received and of my current circumstance. His unconcerned tone only reiterated what he told me next.

"I suggest that you move out of town." End of conversation. What else could this dysfunctional town throw at me?

I decided that the best thing for me to do was to move back to the farm. I could get away from that town every night after work and recoup from whatever the day had thrown at me. I discussed this idea with Mom to make sure that Dad would have no objections. The arrangements were set. I contacted my landlord and explained the situation. He was not pleased, and he informed me that I would lose my deposit. I agreed. All I could think of was getting the hell out of that miserable town. It was only twenty-five miles from work, and the kids and I could continue my scheduled visits. I thought the farm would be good for the children also. Grandma spoiled them and they loved going to the farm. I hoped it would provide some solution to this excruciating environment.

Lord, are you there? I wasn't quite sure anymore. I continued going to church with Mom and Dad, but people weren't treating me very kindly. Some of Mom and Dad's friends even started giving them the cold shoulder. One of the older ladies in the church, Gladys, even told Mom that they should turn their back on me and my sinful lifestyle. She also added that I was going to burn in hell if I didn't repent of my sin and purge this abomination from my soul. I didn't understand how Christians could be so cold and uncaring. At a time when I needed my church family, they ridiculed, judged, and crucified me. I was no longer a pillar of the community but made to feel like the scum of the earth with no value or credibility.

It didn't matter any longer. I had lost everything but my job and even that was precarious at best. I became convinced that God didn't love me anymore; after all, His church hated me. God didn't care what I was going through. I totally denied His faithfulness and His promises that He made me earlier in my life. My spirit was scarred and broken. My heart grew cold towards people. Nobody loved me anymore.

Chapter 14

There is Power in the Blood

For the life of the flesh is in the blood:
for it is the blood that maketh atonement for the soul.

Leviticus 17:11 (KJV)

Tony and I met in my senior year of high school. He was in the new junior class below me, but we shared our drafting lab. He was a tall, slender young man with a bright future. He was smart and later became the top draftsman of his class. We quickly became best friends and shared many accomplishments together.

After graduation Tony married his high school sweetheart. Much to my surprise, Tony was hired at the same company where I was working as a draftsman. Since we were friends in school, and he and his wife living not far from me, we decided to carpool. We continued working together for about five years. We shared everything during those commutes back and forth and were the best of friends. We shared our Christian faith and our experiences in church. He attended a different church, but we often enjoyed going to different functions with each other and our wives.

Tony and I remained friends after I started a new job with a different company. He was elected as a trustee for his church but soon experienced dissention from the older board members. It was common for growing churches to experience this, but these old codgers were very obstinate. Tony's church was floundering because of the constant bickering in board meetings that carried over into attitudes during worship.

One Sunday morning, about the same time I was experiencing so much turmoil at church, Tony and his wife came to my church. I assumed he had heard rumors about Mona and me divorcing, but he never asked. They sat in the pew in front of me, and we exchanged small talk before service started. I noticed that Tony's wife was acting a bit peculiar. She leaned toward her husband, a few whispers, then

"Turn to page 191 in your hymnal." You could hear pages turning throughout the auditorium.

The music started.

"Would you be free from your burden of sin?
There's pow'r in the blood. Pow'r in the blood.
Would you o'er evil a victory win?
There's wonderful pow'r in the blood.
There is pow'r, pow'r, wonder working pow'r,
In the blood of the Lamb.
There is pow'r, pow'r, wonder working pow'r,
In the precious blood of the Lamb."

Suddenly, I noticed Tony's wife nudge him on the arm. She grabbed her purse and glanced my way with a disapproving look, as they started moving toward the aisle. Tony intentionally ignored my attempt to make eye contact. I watched them as I continued singing, wondering what was wrong. They didn't leave; instead they moved to a pew a few rows up in front of me. *Was it me? What was that look all about? It had to be me, it just had to be.*

Why else would she give me that look? She didn't like me talking to her husband? I could instantly feel my face turn red. I was embarrassed. I felt humiliated. I felt the eyes of everyone around me, as if they were burning a hole through my skull.

Mom noticed that something was wrong. We rode together to church and the ride home was painful. She asked me what was wrong and I started to cry.

"You look like you just lost your best friend," she said.

"I did," I replied.

"What happened?" she asked as she turned toward me in the front seat.

"I don't know, but I think Tony's wife has a problem with me."

We discussed my feelings for a little while, then, my mother said something that never occurred to me. She explained that the younger people in the church had not lived long enough to understand the circumstances which arise in life we sometimes have no control over. It not only helped explain Tony's wife's reaction, but it also gave me some insight into my mother's hidden psychology. I started to understand that she may not agree with my lifestyle, but she did have compassion and empathy for my pain.

"I'm done!" I proclaimed. "Why am I beating my head up against a wall? It doesn't matter to these people what I'm going through. All they want to do is judge, condemn, and punish me. That isn't God. That isn't Christianity. It's just plain mean. I'll never go back. I'm through!" I wept as I drove.

My mother and father were silent. I knew they understood. They saw the pain and injustice. Little did I know that this moment had a profound affect on my father.

I became bitter at God. I didn't understand how God could allow His children or His church to behave this way. The resentment that was building in my heart was undeniable. How could these people who professed to be compassionate, mature Christians, treat someone they had known for fifteen years this way? They were hypocrites. I didn't need people like them in my life. God would just have to understand.

Stephen and I met at a birthday party for a mutual friend. We immediately clicked in a way I had never experienced. I felt free to finally explore my homosexual these feelings and so I did! Stephen and I talked for hours. I discovered that he had recently separated from his wife and had many unresolved issues concerning his wife, much like myself. We talked about religion and my recent experience with the church. We talked about our children. His two boys were sixteen and eighteen. We discovered so many things we had in common, and he was pretty easy on the eyes too.

The next day at work, I received roses. Boy did that get my co-workers talking. I thought it was funny. I don't know why, other than the fact that I had never received flowers before. I called and thanked Stephen for his kind gesture and asked if he would like to meet me for lunch. He accepted. I couldn't wait to see him again. The lunch lasted for three hours.

Our friendship quickly turned into a relationship. And our relationship quickly turned into gossip. There were so many people who knew both of us; it didn't take long for people to put two and two together. It also didn't take long for some to ask nosey questions. I just took it in stride; after all, I was starting to get used to being talked about. Although, the strangest twist to it all was the fact that Stephen worked with and sat next to the man who was now dating my ex-wife.

After some time I decided I wanted Stephen to meet my parents. I was still living at the farm, so I asked Mom if I could invite him to dinner. She said she wanted to meet him also. Stephen accepted. I wondered if Dad was ready. I guess I would find out.

Both Mom and Dad were very cordial towards Stephen. After meeting him Dad retired to the sofa to watch television (as usual), and Mom finished preparing the meal. I took Stephen on a tour of the farm. We no longer had horses, but I learned that his parents had horses on their farm where he was raised. When we returned to the living room, Stephen noticed the Hammond organ sitting in the corner. He asked if he could play it.

I replied, "I don't know, can you?"

"Ha Ha", he chuckled.

My mother must have fallen in love with him right then and there. She instantly came in from the kitchen and started singing the lyrics to the song he was playing. When he finished, they turned toward each other and smiled warmly at each other. I knew my mother approved. Dad didn't miss a beat, enthralled with the evening news.

Suddenly Dad spouted outrage at the television. "Those people are idiots!" he exclaimed. The evening news was covering a story about Gay Rights. "They just don't understand."

I was shocked, and not many things shocked me anymore. He was actually defending me. I thought to myself, *This speaks volumes.* He was finally understanding that gay people don't choose their lives. They choose to be happy in spite of the hardship. We sat down at the table to eat and had a wonderful dinner. I was pleased because I knew Mom and Dad liked him.

Months had passed, and I was in love. Stephen and I had grown closer and closer, and I loved being with him. I had purchased a small German-brick house and Stephen was helping me remodel. We decide when it was finished, we would move in together. Everything was going smoothly and gossip either moved on to another victim, or we had just gotten used to it. Either way, it seemed as if the stars had aligned in communion with our love for each other.

We soon moved into our newly-remodeled home. It was close to work, and I walked home for lunch everyday. Life was good. Stephen and I were even making plans for a wedding. We knew, of course, that it wasn't legal, but we wanted to celebrate our love for each other. We invited all of our close friends to our celebration. Mutual friends lived in the country and owned a magnificent hundred-year-old home with lovely gardens. We found a minister in Columbus who counseled us and agreed to perform the ceremony.

It was quaint, classy, and private. We invited twenty of our closest friends and had a lovely celebration. My mother and father even came to the reception at my home. It seemed like perfect bliss for a month.

Even though I knew Stephen well since we dated for over a year, there was a definite part of his personality that was very authoritarian. He treated his children with command and offered no leeway in their consideration. He never used this treatment on me, but on one occasion it manifested itself completely.

His youngest son had just started a vocational training program in Law Enforcement and he came to his father for money to purchase uniforms. As Stephen was explaining how child support paid for these things; I waked out of the kitchen area to give them privacy. The argument grew as Stephen exclaimed that it was not his responsibility to pay for these items, but rather his mother's duty. The next thing I knew, there was a rumbling and scuffling, and the sound of my refrigerator jarring, and a loud thud onto the floor. I jolted back to the kitchen to find Stephen restraining his son in a half nelson body hold with his son underneath him on the floor. I was appalled. I immediately ordered Stephen off his son and he quickly released him from his grip. The boy stood up and ran out of the house screaming obscenities at his father. Stephen sat in rest at the disheveled kitchen table.

"What in the hell did you think you were doing?" I yelled. I was furious with him. He sat in silence without even looking me in the eye. I could tell that he knew that he had crossed a line. Stephen was fully aware of the abuse in my past, and he also knew I would never tolerate it in my home.

The parallels to Jett came rushing back into my mind as if they had happened yesterday. Those little videos that I ran through my brain came flooding back with vivid images. I couldn't help but feel that familiar feeling of helplessness and betrayal from those many years earlier.

I was extremely disappointed in Stephen. In fact, I believed that the violation of my home was unforgivable. Within weeks of the incident, I asked Stephen to pack his belongings and leave. It wasn't worth the heartache. It was over. His actions killed my love for him, and I was done.

The closure was abrupt and final. I wanted nothing more to do with him. The disappointment and heartbreak were more than I was comfortable dealing with. Little by little I began running to the bars. The difference in atmosphere was quite welcome. It was easy within the gay community to become "loose and fancy free," and I put myself in some very precarious situations. "Anything goes" is pretty much the norm. I found some of the gay culture absolutely repulsive; nonetheless, there I was in the midst of the debauchery.

One particular evening, while cruising for some company at a local park, I met a man and went home with him. We had our fun; then, he put me up in a spare bedroom to sleep. I thought it was rather odd that he wouldn't let me sleep with him, but I dismissed it. The room was in the back of the house with one small window. It was comfortable but somewhat drab. I undressed and crawled under the covers for a much—needed sleep. As I was lying in bed, twilight came over me; I was still awake but in a dream state. My consciousness suddenly changed, and right before my eyes were the hands of Jesus. He showed me the scars in His hands and proclaimed to me, by saying my name, that He was who He was. Jesus was actually speaking to me. *Is this real? What is going on?* Instantly He showed me the room I was in, but only from His perspective. He showed me I could easily be trapped in the room if the narrow doorway were blocked. I somehow knew that the window was screwed shut. Then, as if from a scene in *A Christmas Carol*, I was a bystander. I saw in the vision this man arrive at the doorway with a shotgun. I knew his intent, and I was not leaving the room, except in a body bag.

I was quickly stirred as if something pushed me in my bed. I sat straight up completely alert and ready. NO TIME TO QUESTION THIS! I jumped out of bed and into my clothes. I quickly dashed into my shirt and harpooned my shoes with my toes. I grabbed my jacket, made sure I had my wallet, and darted down the hall. When I ran into the kitchen toward the back door, much to my dismay, there he was, awake, sitting at his kitchen table. I made a quick excuse and left as quickly as I possibly could. I never saw the man again.

I continued participating in this type of behavior for many months. Some were "tricks," and some I dated for a while. Some took advantage of me. Some stole money. Many lied, deceived, and one gave me something I can never forget.

Three Months Later

I had showered and shaved as I usually do without notice of anything unusual about my face. I went into work late because it was Friday morning, and it was customary to take any comp time earned on Fridays. I arrived at my office and went about preparing my first task of the day. I made my coffee and sat down to my computer to start working. I noticed my stomach was upset and not liking my coffee very well. I was nauseated. I tried to shake it off, but soon found myself in the men's room upchucking my breakfast. I had no explanation for this. I looked up in the mirror and noticed that a red rash overtaken my complexion. *What was this?* I retreated to my office and closed my door. I finished my task that I had started, then called my secretary and informed her that I was not feeling well and was going home.

I left work and went home, straight to bed. Chills were overcoming my body and cuddling up in my warm bed was all I wanted. I fell fast asleep.

I woke to a burning fever. I scrambled for the thermometer. I cleaned it and inserted it under my tongue. I was weak. I could hardly stand. *What is wrong with me?* My temperature was 104.2. *Oh My*! I called 9-1-1.

By the time paramedics arrived, my heart was racing. The first thing the medic did was take my blood pressure.

"Heart Rate's 140. Blood pressure 162 over 100, respiration thirty-two."

My Eyes were closed. I could sense that the paramedic was quickly trying to insert an IV into my arm. They lifted me from my bed onto a guerney. Then, I felt the rumble of the wheels and a lift out the back door. I could feel the cold February air on my face. In my mind's eye I could see Mother's face. It was warm and kind, as if she were extremely peaceful. My body was tingling. Everything was changing quickly. I could no longer think from my brain; instead I could feel my thinking shift from my head to my torso. Strange but true. All of the life within my body was being collected into my bellybutton area. Visions started encompassing my thoughts. I saw Travis graduating. He was accepting his diploma. I was experiencing the joy of the moment. Suddenly, I was walking Ashley down the aisle, her face covered with a veil; I felt nervous, but proud to be at her side. It was a happy moment filled with peace and love. "Heart Rate fourteen. Hurry!"

I could hear scrambling made by the paramedics. Plastic ripping open.

"Nitro." We need to go."

I remember being put in the squad and needing two more doses of nitro.

Emergency Room. They took many blood samples. I was sleepy. *Just let me sleep. Someone turn the volume down. Let me sleep.*

"Hi Ellen! When did you get here?"

The doctor entered my cubicle. "Your blood work is all over the map. What have you been doing lately? he asked with a rather confused expression on his face.

"Me? I got really sick this morning." I replied.

"Yes, I would agree. You almost died. I want to schedule a stress test and chase a few rabbits with your blood-work. The nurse will be in to take some more blood. In the meantime, you just rest but no sleeping." He left as quickly as he came.

"Did he say . . . NO sleeping! Great! Ellen, I don't know what happened. I started getting sick at work and broke out with this rash on my face. Is it still there?"

"Yes," she replied.

"Did he say what my temperature was?"

"102," she replied.

"What the hell is happening!"

Several hours passed and they admitted me for testing. I was exhausted. All I wanted to do was sleep. Ellen sat by my side. I could tell she was deeply concerned as she continued to ask questions about how I was feeling. A nurse came in and informed me I was scheduled for a stress test the following morning. I fell asleep.

The next morning they woke me and prepared me for testing. I was so weak. I couldn't manage walking so they performed a chemical reaction test which manipulates the heart rate. They explained they were totally prepared in case my heart would stop, or in the event of a heart attack, they could stop it. *Thanks, that was comforting!*

They started their procedure and injected something into my IV. I started feeling a tingle at the very top of my head. It slowly flowed down the back of my head and down my forehead to my nose. It continued across my ears and down my neck and shoulders, then my back. My heart started pumping enough that I could feel it in my chest. This was strange, because I felt like I had just walked a mile. My heart continued to increase in rate. I could feel the tingling dissipate around my lower chest. But it kept flowing, wave after wave, down to my heart.

I could feel the blood rushing through my veins in my arms and the back of my knees. My heart continued to gain speed.

"We've reached max. We will stay at this rate for one minute then start reducing the intake." I heard the doctor say.

My heart was racing as if I was running uphill. My breathing started to increase. *Ok, I've had enough. Can you hear me? I can't take anymore.* Nothing was coming out of my mouth. Suddenly, the waves of chemical slowed and my heart responded. Gradually my heart rate was slowed until it reached normal a few minutes later. The results showed that my heart was normal. *Thanks . . . You were a cheap date*!, again nothing coming out of my mouth.

They took me back to my room after a brief monitoring period. I was exhausted. *Just let me sleep.* Just then, the doctor came into my room.

"We have some results. It's not good news.

"You're HIV positive."

Time stood still.

Chapter 15

Irises and Geraniums

"Whew!" I could have been knocked over with a feather. The world actually stopped spinning, as I tried to comprehend what the doctor had just said. I felt warped, sick, nauseated. *Oh My! Now what do I do?* The reality just hadn't fully hit me yet. It felt like my body was trying to catch up with time that was just lost.

"You're experiencing Acute Sero-conversion, which means your body is fighting an acute HIV Infection. The rash is caused by the virus and usually starts with the head and then spreads to the chest. It will go away in a week or so. Your test is positive, and your body is just now coming under attack by the virus. Sometimes this happens immediately upon being infected—sometimes it's weeks, even years. Some barely show any signs or have symptoms like the flu. Yours was intensified by a panic attack which caused the reduction of heart function. Your liver is functioning completely erratically, but we expect it to stabilize within a few weeks. You will be under observation for a couple of days while you regain your strength. I'll see you again before you're released." He left the room.

I was alone. I was by myself, with myself and nobody else. My thoughts were racing, not focusing on anything, just scrambling from one thought to another. Nothing I was thinking was making sense. *What are you going to do now, Jon? Sleep! Just sleep.*

Two Weeks Later

The doctor released me from the hospital after a few days with strict instructions to rest, eat right, and not do anything strenuous. He explained I would feel weak for several weeks, and I was not allowed to return to work for three months. I completed the necessary paperwork for my employer and focused on recovering. I soon discovered that the smell of food made me nauseated. I couldn't cook anything without getting sick. I couldn't eat fast-food unless it was cold, so I started eating cold foods and cold foods only! I only went out in public when I had to restock supplies and that was all. Every night I would wake in a pool of sweat, drenched and chilled, getting up in the middle of the night to change my sheets. I looked like I had been run over by a Mack truck. Mona and I made arrangements to adjust my visitation schedule while I was recuperating. I didn't tell her what was wrong, only that I had a viral infection. I was so weak. For weeks it took my breath to walk from one end of the house to the other. I was wiped out all of the time.

Mom had not been feeling well either. Dad had just had a prostatectomy after a cancer diagnosis. The doctor removed the prostate and confirmed the cancer had not spread. The stress from the situation worried Mom to the point that she developed angina. I didn't have the heart to tell Mom what I was dealing with. Ellen knew but promised she would keep my secret.

I decided I would go and visit Mom and Dad for a few hours. I was feeling a bit better and thought a visit would do us all good. Mom had been spending a lot of time in bed, as her condition made any activity very straining. The house was a bit disheveled and needed cleaning. Mom's plants needed tending. She loved Irises and Geraniums and wintered them in her living room. Four large picture windows provided a plethora of light, and they thrived, even in the midst of winter. Mom loved her flowers, and oh, how they rewarded her. Her flowers would bloom with brilliant bursting flowers.

It was very refreshing after the past few weeks to see something living in such a bleak cold winter. I went about cleaning and straightening the house, fixing a light dinner, and doing some laundry. Mom stayed in bed and gave me instructions when needed. Dad watched a ball game the entire time. When it came time to leave, Mom got out of bed and came to the foyer in her robe and slippers. She thanked me for all I did and gave me a big hug. I loved Mom's hugs. She would just engulf me with warmth while she was pulling me in tight. There's nothing like a hug from Mom.

I spent the time driving home in deep thought. I was on autopilot as I managed turns and traffic lights. I wondered if I should have told them. I just couldn't. Mom had enough on her mind, and I certainly wasn't going to add to it. I just kept thinking about my dreams and aspirations. I couldn't help but think they were dead. There was nothing to look forward to now but deteriorating health. *How long before it turned into Aids? What did all of those numbers mean that the doctor talked about? When would I get my strength back? How in the world do I tell my family?*

What would my kids do without a father? I felt completely emptied of all emotions, but I must have felt something because a tear slid down my cheek. I should have never let this happened. I blamed no one but myself. I felt tainted and poisoned. I kept thinking about the blood running through my veins, and it just felt poisoned. *Nobody will want to be around me. I have to educate myself about this disease. I don't want to infect my children or loved ones. But how do I do all of that? I need to find out more. I must figure out a way to keep going.* I kept hearing a whistle in my head. It wouldn't stop.

I woke the next morning determined to learn about this virus inside my body. I didn't understand why the doctor didn't put me on any medication. I needed to learn how this virus worked, but where do I obtain this information. It's not like there was a hotline I could call. I had heard of others who had died from this; I must stop that from happening. *What about my children? What about my future with them?* I decided to contact the Center for Disease Control (CDC), in Atlanta, and discovered that there was a hotline for HIV/AIDS.

I arrived home late. I had been out running errands all day. There had been a lot that I had neglected, including food, which had been the least of all my concerns; nonetheless, I had to maintain my health. I was very weak and vulnerable. I had no more strength. I was exhausted. I felt like I had no fight or hope left—physically, mentally, emotionally and spiritually. Little did I know the storm was just gaining strength.

I went to the bedroom to check my messages. The first one was from Ellen. "Beep . . . . Jon pick-up." Call as soon as you get this!"

Next message.

In a distraught weeping voice, "Beep . . . . Jon, I need you."

I was puzzled. I thought for a moment that it was Stephen, but no.

Next message. "Beep . . . . This is Berger Hospital. We're trying to locate the son of Lillian. Please contact us as soon as possible. The number is . . . ###-####." Click!

The machine wouldn't quit resetting fast enough. I called the number left on the message and reached the Emergency Room receptionist.

"Hello, this is Jon Lewis, and there was a message left for me to contact the hospital. Is this concerning my mother Lillian?"

"Just a minute please and you can speak to the doctor."

The doctor's voice came the phone, "Yes, is this Jon?"

"Yes," I said.

"I regret to inform you that your mother passed away this evening. I'm so sorry . . . ."

I started screaming!

I threw the phone across the room,

"No! No! No! This can't be!"

Sobbing overtook me completely. I wailed uncontrollably. I couldn't stop. My grieving continued without pause for twenty minutes or so. I had never felt such devastation and complete despair. My constitution had been crushed with utter finality.

After I collected my composure, I called Ellen. She was somber and silent but told me Dad was with her and spending the night. I told her I was on my way but I was going to stop by the hospital first. I left quickly.

I arrived at the emergency room doors. They opened automatically, and I approached the reception desk. I told the woman who I was, and she remembered talking to me. I asked her to see if it was possible for me to see my mother's body. She wasn't sure, but she immediately left to inquire about my request. The night shift doctor soon appeared from the double doors to the treatment rooms. We talked for a few minutes, and he agreed to let me see mom. He informed me she was an organ donor, and they were in the process of harvesting her corneas, as they must perform this procedure before the body temperature dropped. I found a seat in the empty waiting room. The lights were darkened, and shades were pulled as if to speak to my spirit in dim accord. I waited, quietly sobbing. It wouldn't stop. I was alone; abandoned by the only source of secure understanding I had ever known. I could feel the stone foundations of my soul crumbling.

The doctor soon arrived in the waiting room to escort me back to where my mother's body was. The curtains were pulled around her. He pointed then turned and left. I was alone with my mother's dead body separated only by a curtain. I paused for a moment with an overwhelming feeling of grief. For a brief moment I wondered if I was ready to see her but knew I would regret it if I didn't. I pulled back the veil to reveal my mother lying on a gurney. A sheet covered her body except her arms, shoulders, and head. White gauze patches covered her eyes as she lay there with her mouth gaping open. I grabbed her hand and clasped her fingers with mine. Her body was only lukewarm, but it was almost as if she would return the caress at any moment. I looked at her hair, her cheeks, and her lips as a hollowed feeling overcame me. Huge tears fell from my eyes and rested on her face then gently rolled down her cheek. I wiped them with my thumb, touching her face for the last time. I leaned over and carefully placed a kiss on her forehead and I could smell her lifeless breath coming from her open mouth. I wanted her to hug me. I wanted her to sit up and tell me that everything was going to be all right. I longed for the impossible but realized the certainty. I dropped my head as I took one last look at my precious friend, confidant, and teacher. I turned and left without looking at or speaking to anyone. I sat in my cold car in a dark empty parking lot sobbing; sobbing without end.

I pulled into Ellen's driveway, and she opened the front door. I greeted her with an inconsolable hug. Both of us were crying in the cold night air. She took me upstairs to where Dad was resting. I could smell Mom's scent. The aroma was strong, as Dad mentioned it when I arrived at his bedside. I embraced him, he cried in my arms.

The entire family met at the funeral home to discuss arrangements. Jett and his wife, Will, and his son Brian was there. Ellen was by herself, and I was alone also. I was angry. I was angry at God for taking her so soon. I felt to blame because of my HIV. I had spent the last twenty-fours hours feeling responsible that God took her to spare her the grief, agony, and shame of dealing with my disease. Ellen was still the only person who knew about the stay in the hospital, and it was our secret. I had no intention of telling anyone.

The tension in the room was like heavy-laden snow. Jett didn't speak, and I made no attempt to communicate either. We hadn't seen each other in several years. We talked about the normal arrangements and what Dad wanted for the funeral. By the time it came to pick out the casket, I was primed to cut loose. It only took a few comments from Jett's wife to set me off. As we were looking at the various crypts, Jett's wife started making statements about which one she liked the best. *She could care less what Mom would like.* It was more than I could take. It was like a bomb went off in me which made the consequences seem trivial.

As everyone left the room, Will, Jett, and I were the last ones out of the room. I turned to Jett, pointed in his face and quite plainly let him know how I felt about his wife being present. I blamed Tammy for Jett's withdraw from the family. Our mutual animosities erupted as he immediately drew back his hand in a fist and aimed it straight at my face. Will grabbed Jett's forearm and stopped him mid swing from striking me. I looked him in the eye and turned and walked out of the room. I was so upset. I needed air. I stood outside for what seemed like an hour. I felt so alone. This was a gap that nobody could possibly fill. My mother was gone. My best friend had died. The emptiness consumed me. Ellen came and retrieved me.

We sat in the foyer discussing how I was doing. I wanted to say that inside I was doing terrible, but I kept my mouth shut. I really didn't want to discuss my health at that moment, but her presence was a comfort. Soon Dad joined us and asked if I was all right. He told me that he understood how hard this was and proclaimed we could all get through this. He stood up and invited me back to the conference room. I followed.

When I entered the room, I approached Jett and he extended his open hand. I reached for his shoulder and pulled him into a hug. Will put his arms around both of us, and we all cried together.

Mom was buried in a quaint country cemetery that overlooks the ridge where the farm is located. It is situated in the rolling Hocking Hills facing east with pine groves, huge oak trees, and stately headstones. That following spring I planted Irises and Geraniums. I can feel her gentle spirit each time I visit. I miss her terribly.

I spent the next several weeks intensely grieving and mourning my mother. There were many days I felt lonely and depressed. My mood was always somber and pissed off. It seemed untrue, and like it shouldn't have happened.

My anger at God worsened as I was dealing with the unfair reality of her death. God was silent and it felt as though He didn't care about me at all. How cruel to let me sink into this pit of hell. No extended arm of salvation for me. It felt as if Satan were tempting me: "Cross this gap, just try and cross this gap."

The stress from the loss caused a temporary paralysis on the right side of my face called Bells Palsy. I couldn't talk without a lisp, and it became even more difficult to eat. The muscles on the right side of my face would not function. I couldn't chew. I lost quite a bit of weight and dropped to weighing 150 pounds with a 29-inch waist.

Chapter 16

One Too Many

The sacrifices of God are a broken spirit,
A broken and contrite heart.
O God, you will not despise.

Psalm 51:17 (NIV)

There was a knock at the door. As I opened it, Dad was standing there, and I could sense that he had been crying. A couple of months had passed since Mom's death and I knew Dad was having a difficult time. Mom was always concerned about Dad's welfare if anything should happen to her. He had suffered a mental breakdown several years earlier when he lost his job. And Dad was not the type to care for himself even when times were good. He was now alone, cooking, cleaning, washing laundry, and caring for the farm. It was a major adjustment for him that he was not handling well. His grieving was obvious, and he would commence crying whenever talking about mom.

I had not yet told him of my diagnosis, but I knew I couldn't keep it a secret forever. The timing was awful because I really didn't want to add any more stress, but he was curious about my drastic weight loss. I was still eating cold foods, and I was running out of options for a healthy diet. It was getting more and more difficult to manage my weight, and my doctor really didn't give me any good advice except to eat as many fatty foods as I could. My face was quickly becoming emaciated—not a healthy look for someone only thirty-four.

I welcomed Dad into the living room where he sat in a wingback chair across from me. We chatted for a while, mostly about the adjustments that he was not managing well. Then, he asked me about my weight and what was wrong with my face and speech. Although I didn't want to, I knew this was the best time to inform him of my condition. I explained to him what the doctor had told me about the palsy. I told him that it was triggered by the stress of Mom's death, but the underlying cause was HIV. He started to cry. Wiping tears from his face, he asked when I found out and if I knew who gave me the disease. I informed him of the hospital stay; that I did know the person who infected me, but the blame belonged to me. It took a while, but he composed himself and told me how very sorry he was.

"Dad, I've been thinking. What if I sold this house and moved back to the farm so we could take care of each other? I know you need help and I could use the time to catch my breath."

He replied, "If that's what you want to do, it's fine with me."

We embraced with a warm hug and he left.

The next day I contacted a realtor and put the house on the market. It sold in four weeks, and I put most of my belongings in storage. I moved a few items and all of my personal necessities to the farm. Oh, how I loved the farm. It was strange to be there without Mom. I could feel her presence everywhere on that hilltop. It was late spring, and the dogwood trees and lilacs were in bloom. I could smell their sweet aroma everywhere I went. It brought me so much comfort to know, at the very least, I was surrounded by what she loved.

It was Mother's Day weekend, and Jett and his family made an unexpected visit to the farm. I had not yet told Jett of my disease. Instinct told me to keep it quiet for the time being. Jett became inquisitive about my failing health. He then stated that I probably had Aids and killed Mom with the news of the disease. Then, he said that I probably wouldn't live to see my fortieth birthday. I just shook my head and went into the house. I couldn't believe the words I heard come from my brother's mouth, and his young children were present. I was heartbroken.

Several weeks passed and I had been contemplating telling Jett the truth. It just didn't matter to me if he thought I killed my mother because it just wasn't the truth. He could think whatever he wanted to; it wouldn't be the first time I was blamed for something I didn't do. By chance, he called the farm to talk to Dad. I told Dad I was going to tell Jett the truth, so Dad handed me the phone.

"Jett, there's something I need to tell you," I stated.

"Yea, what?"

"I'm HIV positive, and I thought you might want to know."

"Okay. Thanks for telling me. Let me talk to Dad," he replied.

I handed Dad the phone with a puzzled expression on my face. There was no screaming, no chastisement, no nothing. I was stunned. I left the room while Dad and Jett finished their conversation.

Dad came out on the front porch where I was sitting.

"Get a load of this!" he proclaimed. He then proceeded to tell me that Jett lambasted him for not informing him about me. He felt I jeopardized his children when he last visited. Dad informed him that he needed to be educated about the disease and not jump to conclusions. I told Dad I was proud of him but sorry for the berating.

The doctor had not yet released me to return to work, so I spent the days enjoying the farm and taking care of Dad. It wasn't long before a widow at church took an interest in him. He seemed to enjoy her company, and it didn't take long for them to develop a relationship. They were soon planning a September wedding.

My recuperation was taking longer than I expected during which time my washing machine quit working. I went to our local home improvement store to see what was available. The store salesman was very handsome. After completing the sale he gave me a very deliberate, connecting smile. He was flirting with me! With the way I looked, I couldn't imagine anyone being interested. I just blew it off, as I was in no position to start any kind of relationship.

But one day, Dad needed to run into town to pick up a part he needed for the mower. As we were walking through the store, I caught the eye of this man again. He immediately walked over to us and asked if he could be of assistance. Dad just walked off, but I stayed and started a conversation with him. His name was Rick. He told me he was glad to see me again and asked a personal question. I answered him positively, and his response definitely told me he was gay. He said he would like to get together sometime and get a bite to eat. I responded with a smile; he proceeded to write down his phone number. We shook hands affectionately, and I walked off with a chipper strut.

I was very unsure if I should call Rick. My disease made it very difficult to even think of being in a relationship with someone. *How would he react? Can I face this probable rejection?*

A few days passed, then I decided to call him. We made arrangements to meet at a restaurant in the town where he lived. We had a wonderful dinner, sharing many stories and getting to know each other. He was from a small town, but had a big family in West Virginia. Rick was no stranger to tragedy as he lost a brother to a car accident a few years earlier and his father to alcoholism. He moved to Ohio after graduating from West Virginia Tech with a degree in Music Education. He promised he would sing for me sometime, and I looked forward to it.

We ended the evening sitting and talking on his front porch. I kept waiting for the right moment to tell him about my disease. I waited and waited, but the conversation wasn't presenting an opportunity until I finally just blurted it out. It was so out-of-sync with our conversation but I had to get it out. I did not expect his reaction. He replied that it didn't matter if it's the right person. Well, he got my vote right then and there. He explained to me that it was possible that he could be HIV positive too, but had not been tested for some time. He went on to tell me, as a gay man, he accepted the possibility a long time ago. I found his honesty to be refreshing and thought, if nothing else, I had found a friend. I was surprised when the evening ended with a gentle kiss.

Within a week Rick and I were discussing living together. It seemed a fit for both of us, so we started looking for an apartment together. We soon moved in and bought furniture together. I considered the pitfalls, but Rick's sweet and gentle personality comforted my doubts. I instinctively trusted him, which didn't come easily for me. Even though he worked hard and had a good job, he wasn't good at managing money, so we immediately worked on getting him out of debt.

I soon returned to work. Unfortunately, it was not a pleasant experience. It wasn't long before I discovered everyone knew about my HIV. Some of my coworkers were not silent about their displeasure of my presence in the office. Someone made a crude joke about gays in a staff meeting while my boss was out of the room. Many guys would turn and walk out of the men's restroom if they saw me there. And worse yet, someone scratched on a bathroom stall wall, "Fuckin Queer Die". Even people outside of the Engineering Department would say, "He's the one with Aids!" as they pointed at me. Someone even stole my nameplate above my office door as a humiliating joke. Others would turn the other way if I was coming toward them in the hallway.

I had never felt so demoralized, vulnerable, and insecure in my entire life. I had a very difficult time understanding how people could be so cruel. I was even asked not to make coffee any longer. I couldn't have been more humiliated. I continued doing my job as best I could under the circumstances, but I finally had to have a meeting with my boss. I told him the behavior of my coworkers was unacceptable, and I would hold him accountable if he didn't put a stop to their behavior. He had a very indignant attitude, but he did attempt to control the harassment.

My work environment seemed to be deteriorating at a fast pace. I began to dread going to work. Every day, someone would make an issue of my illness in one way or the other. People seemed obsessed to make my life very difficult and uncomfortable. The stress was already making me crack. I was soon off work again for exhaustion.

The stress from work was taking its toll. I was running fevers, experiencing excruciating headaches, and not sleeping. The burden of this disease was destroying me. The doctor finally thought it necessary to start me on an anti-viral medicine called AZT. There was only two medications available, and this one was the most effective. My doctor monitored my blood work, and my viral load was in the hundreds of thousands. In clinical terms this meant that when one drop of blood was measured, there were that many copies of the virus multiplying themselves, which explained how the virus was ravaging my body. My skin was turning a pale gray color, and I looked like death warmed over. Just months before, I would have never dreamed that my life would have become this pitiful. *How could anybody want to be a part of this decrepitation?*

Rick stood by me through this horrendous time for a while, but it took its toll on us also. Rick started coming home later and later from work. My job was so taxing that I was too exhausted to deal with the possibility of what he might be doing behind my back, and I didn't have the energy to care. I was very sick. *What was next? I couldn't take any more.* He constantly made messes, which he refused to clean up. He became increasingly difficult to live with. It wasn't long before we became estranged.

Rick had received a promotion, and he was doing educational training for new employees. He was traveling good distances every day and wasn't home much. He would come in late at night and sleep in the recliner in the living room, covering with a fleece throw. I saw him very seldom and we never shared a meal any more.

At Thanksgiving, Rick was scheduled to train employees at a new store located two hours away. He informed me he would be staying in a hotel while he was getting this new operation started. He started badgering me about my inability to keep the apartment clean. My opposition to his opinion, given the fact that he was the slob who didn't clean up his messes, only infuriated him more. Furthermore, he didn't seem to grasp the fact that I was too sick to live up to his expectations. I packed my suitcase and personals and left the apartment in a fury.

I drove to the farm where Dad and his new wife welcomed me—I think mostly out of pity. Nonetheless I felt at home again. The comfort of this place helped ease the pain of what just happened, and I figured I would just stay while Rick was away. I was driving back and forth to work, and once again, after a day's work, I was glad to drive up the ridge over the hills and dales to a place of solace.

A week passed and I had not heard from Rick. I deduced from his statement he would be home that next weekend, and I was too stubborn to contact him first.

Monday, while at work, I received a phone call. The receptionist gave me a message for the call to be returned. She stated that it was urgent. The woman's name didn't ring a bell at first, but I called the number that was given. It was Rick's sister.

"Hello, this is Jon. I'm returning your call."

The voice on the other end replied, "This is Debby, Rick's sister. I hate to have to tell you this but, Rick was killed in a car accident last night."

"Where? How?" I gasped.

"He was only a half mile from home when he fell asleep at the wheel and went under a semi-truck as it was passing him. It killed him instantly."

"Oh, my God! Oh, my God! Oh, my God! What can I do?" I asked.

"I'll contact you when we have funeral arrangements made." she replied.

"Thank you for calling me, Debby. I'm so sorry. Please give your mother my condolences."

I slowly hung up the phone. I dropped my head to my desk, trying to absorb what I had just been told. I looked up and there stood a co-worker in my doorway.

I could tell by the look on his face he had overheard my conversation. He apologized and asked if there was anything he could do. I just walked past him in tears and I headed for the bathroom. I gained my composure then went to my secretary and informed her I would be out the rest of the day.

I left work and headed for the apartment we had shared. When I arrived I couldn't help but stare at the empty parking space. I looked at the front door as if I was waiting for it to open, but it never did. My key turned the deadbolt and I stepped inside.

Just inside the front door was his recliner. His blanket throw was neatly folded and placed in the seat. I couldn't help but look at the glass coffee table which was polished spotless. Every VHS tape and DVD was neatly arranged and placed on its proper shelf. I suddenly felt an oppressive weight fall on me and I fell to my knees. I wept uncontrollably as my tears fell to the carpet. I couldn't catch my breath. My head was full as if someone had poured concrete into my brain.

The loss I felt was immense and final. I knew there was no way I could apologize for our argument and no reconciliation could possibly happen. It was done and irreversible.

I pulled myself to my feet, still crying. I walked into the dining room and a piece of paper was lying on the clean glass table. I picked it up and realized it was an itemized budget I had written out for Rick months earlier. I laid it back down and turned to the kitchen to find it completely spotless. There wasn't even one glass in the sink. I didn't understand why the apartment was so pristine, but it didn't matter. Rick was gone.

I drove home listening to Toni Braxton's new CD. "Unbreak My Heart" just kept a lump in my throat like I had never experienced before. I couldn't help but keep hitting the repeat button over and over again. My anguish was growing and completely engulfing me. I made it to Dad's and spent the entire night bawling, while listening to the CD. I felt cursed and abandoned. I started to believe I would live the rest of my life in this chasm, a gap without any closure in sight.

The hurt was so complete, and I had a nagging feeling in my gut that I couldn't shake. I discovered where Rick's truck was located and decided to go see it. I asked my best friend Parker to go along for moral support. It was December and snow was covering most of everything, but the sight I beheld when we arrived was absolutely horrible. The front of the truck was completely gone and the windshield also. Upon closer inspection, I could tell where the truck chassis came to rest on top of the driver's cavity. I spotted his glasses, broken in half, lying on the floor-well, which was full of frozen blood two inches deep. Rick's blood, Rick's glasses.

Why did this happen? He was a half mile from home. Why was the apartment in such immaculate condition? It was almost as if he was trying to tell me something. Could he have known he would never be home again? What if he just discovered he was HIV and couldn't live with it? Would Rick take his own life? This pondering and projecting would not end. *Was I to blame for this?* This conjecture was shaking me to my core. The guilt was laid at my feet like a heavy stone. So I picked up the stone and started carrying it.

The next six months brought deep depression and tremendous despair. I had to quit working. My nerves were on their last edge, and my life was once again torn and shredded apart. It felt like the rug had been pulled out from underneath me, again. My balance and all peace was gone. The images of Rick's death just continued to pierce through me. I was put on heavy anti-depressant medications, which made me not give a care to anything. My soul was depleted. I had nothing else to give. Maybe I should just give up too.

No Wait! That's the easy way out. If Rick did commit suicide, it was his actions and not mine. He was the one who chose that way out of this world instead of facing his fears. What about the pain he caused to those left behind? What if this just isn't true? I was such an emotional mess, and I knew that I would never learn the answer to those questions.

Chapter 17

My Log Cabin

And you hath he quickened
Who were dead in trespasses and sins.

Ephesians 2:1 (KJV)

The winter was snowy and bitterly cold, and I had imposed upon Dad and his wife too long. My best friend, Parker and I decided to rent his brother's trailer, because I had to keep expenses to a minimum, as I had no income to survive on, only my savings. I had sold my life insurance for a viatical settlement, which was going to take some time. I was in for a long, hard winter, and I had to make sure I was going to survive. In just a few years I had gone from living in a hundred-plus-year-old Victorian thirteen-room house to a tin can with carpet. It was cramped but sufficient.

It was a struggle to keep the heating bill paid. I was lonesome. Princess Diana was killed. I missed my job in spite of all the hell. It was as if I could feel the cold loss of identity. I was depressed. My grieving was still immense. My schedule of constant doctor appointments was weighing on me. My HIV medications were not working, or I had allergic reactions to them. My blood work numbers were always out of whack. Everything was haywire.

I spent many days sleeping and not even bothering to get out of bed. Life was meaningless, and I started contemplating suicide. How could I do it and where? I had picked out a bridge abutment if I could work up the nerve. The doctor had prescribed the maximum dose of anti-depressant, and it didn't seem to be working. I thought about ending it all. For days everything was haunting me, endlessly, and I had no escape.

A check came in the mail from my viatical settlement. It helped in giving me a reprieve from the depression. I could afford to buy my own place within the lower end of the housing market, and I decided to buy a used manufactured home. It had everything I needed, including appliances. I caught up on my child support and started to try and live life again.

It wasn't long before friends found out I had money. And it wasn't long before guys started calling. I had no interest at first, but one guy I had met through Stephen started calling and asking questions about my love life. I explained to George that I had HIV and he promptly told me that he already knew. I was surprised. "And, you're interested?" I asked. We started to see each other on a regular basis.

George turned out to be a drug addict, a liar, a thief and a con-artist. The fact of the matter was I was buying his affections, and he certainly took advantage of me. He talked me into selling my home and moving out of state with him. I told him I would go only if I could stay in contact with my children on a regular basis. He agreed. He had a strange hold over me that I felt powerless against. I didn't understand it, and I couldn't stop him. He took advantage of my desire to ditch this horrible town where I lived. I sold everything in a huge yard sale and off we went—once again leaving the little town which had brought so much pain. I was glad to see it in my rear view mirror.

After several weeks of settling in, I was organizing my paperwork and bills. I needed to catch up after all of the changes. I was thumbing through my checkbook and discovered two checks were missing, carbon copy and all. I didn't want to suspect George, but it was the only logical explanation. I'd noticed he always wanted to get the mail and I let him. I made sure that I picked up the mail when the next statement came, and I found out why he liked getting the mail so much. I discovered George had written two checks totaling over seven hundred and fifty dollars, and he forged my signature. I immediately approached him with my evidence, which led to a denial and a huge fight commenced. My mind and emotions raced back twenty years as if Jett had just beaten me up. I felt empty, betrayed, and confused. I just knew I couldn't live with him.

The following weekend, Dad helped me move back to the farm. We rented a truck, packed up my entire apartment, and drove back to Ohio; everything, including pitiful me with my tail between my legs. Once again, I'd lost my home. I later discovered George had stolen over seven thousand dollars from me, and written four thousand more in forged checks. The authorities in that city had no desire to help me, and, in fact did nothing to prosecute George. They actually wanted to blame me because of my signature (that wasn't mine), on the checks. I hired an attorney to convince the investigator I was innocent. It ruined my credit and my self-esteem. I couldn't believe that I could have been so stupid. I was just out! I had just eight hundred dollars to my name, and the IRS was after three hundred of that because of how George filled out my taxes.

Did you notice? Dad was the one who rescued me. He was the one who plucked me out of my despairing situation and stood in the gap. We spent the next few months really communicating, as I let him stand in my obvious gap. But there was more . . . the best part of this entire story.

I returned to Dad's and the farm a very sick and broken man. George had stolen everything from me. My next doctor's appointment revealed I had reached a milestone with my disease, and it wasn't a good one. My T-cells had dropped below two hundred and the medicines were not working for me. This meant I technically had Aids. The doctor decided to change my medicine again. I had another allergic reaction, which made me so sick I ended up in the emergency room. There was no more hope. I had no more options. I was going to die.

How do I face death? How could I possibly put my life back together from nothing? I'd lost my money. I'd lost my health. I'd lost my dignity. I'd lost my hope. I had absolutely nothing. It was gone, and I had no motivation to look for it. Satan had won. I was at the end and God didn't care about me any more. I was getting what I deserved and the gap had become a chasm that was too wide and too deep. There was no way I was going to live through this. The road had come to an end, and I was tired of the pain. I was sick and tired of being sick and tired. I was ready to give up.

Then, my eleven-year-old daughter, wrote me a poem, which reminded me why I should fight.

<u>I Need You To Be There</u>

I need you to be there to walk me down the aisle.
I need you to be there, so I can see your gleaming smile.
I need you to be there, so I will never be alone.
And I need you to be there, so I can hear your soothing tone.
I need you to be there, so you can catch me when I fall.
And, I need you to be there, because without you, there's no reason to love at all.
I need you to be there, so I can feel your loving touch.
I need you to be there, because your love means so much.
I need you to be there to tell me that everything's going to be all right
And I need you to be there, as I pray to God every night
I need you to be there when I find that special guy.
I need you to be there as the months and years go by.
Dad, I need you to be there to love and guide me.
By Ashley

This poem touched me so very deeply. I wondered if I would be alive to walk my girl down the aisle. I wondered if I would see my son graduate. The visions that I had years earlier when I almost died were vivid in my mind. I wondered why I saw those profound scenes. I felt truly blessed to have my children. The bond was close and extremely attaching. *How could I just give up with this beautiful soul depending upon me?* I didn't know how, but I became determined to fulfill my privileged duty as a father. I just had to . . . some how, some way.

As bad as my health was, I started going to a charismatic church nearby. The pastor was young and energetic. The music was refreshing and his teaching was magnetic. I didn't go often, and certainly didn't tell anybody my story, but I knew that I needed God in my life again. It was all I had left, even though I had walked away from the whole "religious" thing. I understood most Christians didn't like the idea of a gay being in their midst, but I didn't care about their hang ups, even though I kept it a guarded secret. I needed God. I thought it might bring nothing but disappointment, but I was willing to take the risk. I didn't understand how God could forgive me for all of my bad decisions and wrong turns. I had a plethora of sins from my past and a boatload of guilt. I needed God to forgive me, and I needed to forgive myself.

It was late one evening. Someone at church had given me a cassette tape of the pastor's last message, which I had missed. I lay on my bed this quiet evening and began listening to his sermon on Luke 19:1-5 (NIV).

Jesus entered Jericho and was passing through. A man was there by the name of Zacchaeus; he was a chief tax collector and was wealthy. He wanted to see who Jesus *was, but being a short man he could not because of the crowd. So he ran ahead and climbed a sycamore-fig tree to see him, since Jesus was coming that way. When Jesus reached the spot, he looked up and said to him, <u>Zacchaeus, come down immediately. I must stay at your house today.</u>*

As I was listening intently, I started to picture myself as Zacchaeus, as if I were there witnessing what was happening. I imagined myself climbing that tree, hanging on to the branches as Jesus was approaching. The very moment I imagined seeing Jesus for the first time; something wonderful and startling happened to me. My body was instantly engulfed in electricity. My body suddenly felt suspended and consumed all at the same time. I was quickly frightened. As soon as I felt the fear, the Lord said to me,

"It's okay Jon, It's Me."

I lay quietly for as long as it lasted, which was about seven or eight seconds. It was as if I had touched a live 600-volt electrical wire, but it didn't hurt or damage me in any way. *Did that just happen?* I knew Jesus had touched me. I didn't feel different physically right away, but I knew something miraculous had just happened. I fell asleep wonderfully perplexed.

After I fell asleep, an angel stood before me. He was taller than me and dressed in a simple white garment. His voice was soothing, as he displayed this scene before me.

There were ruins of a log cabin. I could tell what it once was, but it was completely destroyed from the foundation up. All of the timbers laid in ruin and debris was everywhere. There was no way it was inhabitable or even remotely considerable to right standing. The stone foundation looked like it was constructed of river rocks, laid one on top of the other and securely connected. The top of the foundation was completely solid and in tact, with all of the debris on top. Then the angel said to me, "The Lord your God has heard your cries. He has sent me to show you this. What is before you is what your life was. But, this is what your life will be."

Immediately the scene switched to a completely erect and beautiful new log cabin. It looked like it was made of strong logs and timbers, as if it were custom built just for me. Oh, how beautiful the sight before me. Just then the angel disappeared. *Oh! wait!, what was your name?* No answer.

I woke remembering everything the Lord did. But I had one big question. I understood the destroyed cabin, and I understood the new life, but how would I make that happen? It was so far from where my life was right then— so distant and unreachable. I had a reborn hope deep inside, but how would I rebuild all that has been destroyed or heal the deep hurt or even cross that immense gap in my life?

Chapter 18

Redemption

I will ransom them from the power of the grave;
I will redeem them from death.

Hosea 13:14 (NIV)

Rejoice, Rejoice, O Christian, lift up your voice and sing. Eternal hallelujahs to Jesus Christ the King. The hope of all who seek Him, the help of all who find. None other is so loving, so good and kind.

This passage comes from a song entitled, "He Lives." And what magnificent blessing and fortune He brought to my life through that healing. It is extremely important to understand the meaning of the scripture reference given above. God ransomed me, or redeemed me by payment (I Corinthians 6:20). The payment was made through Christ's death on the cross (Matthew 20:28). Ephesians 1:7 says, *In whom (Christ) we have redemption through His blood, the forgiveness of sins, according to the riches of His grace.* He took me out of the hands of Satan (Job 2:6), and redeemed me. I didn't ask for it, He chose to do it for me (Ephesians 1:5). God's grace, or unmerited favor, reached into my undeserving life and pulled me from my own destruction, which would have led to my death. To God be the glory!

He truly was living in my life again. I had absolutely no doubt He lives. He brought me new life and much—

needed new hope. Even though I was still destitute, I knew somehow He would make a way for a new life for me. I didn't understand how or when, but once again I had all confidence in The Lord. I could start to dream again as He nourished my soul.

Something had changed in me. My thinking was different, and I was getting my strength back. I didn't look to the future as if it were a big black gapping hole. My countenance was beaming, and my heart was filled. Life was flowing through my veins instead of this ravaging disease with all of its medical necessities and horrible medications. I could feel my body renewing and repairing itself with each new day. The constant pain was gone, and my body was getting stronger every day. I no longer felt the negative gloom over my life; instead I felt a positive perspective and outlook.

I wish I could explain with more descriptive detail just what God did for me, but He took the enormous gap in my life and filled it with His love and grace. He stood right square in the middle of an immense chasm and provided a bridge from where I had been, to where I needed to be. His touch had flashed through every tissue and molecule of my body. He literally put life back into my blood. He gave me power through His shed blood to make mine whole and functioning again. It was easy for Him, and yet so complex and awe inspiring to me at the same time.

Isaiah 53:5 tells us that by His wounds we are healed. He took that destruction upon Himself to make me well. He placed all of the devastation and deterioration of my body and exchanged it for His body on the cross. I had turned my back on Jesus, yet He took all of my wrong doings and consequences of that iniquity to Himself. And, He did it for me! This true example should show people just how powerful and merciful our God is.

I was scheduled for my next doctor appointment the following week. I was enthusiastically looking forward to it. I couldn't wait to tell my doctor what had happened and how God was quickly changing my life. I stopped taking my anti-depressant and the thirty-six pills per day for my HIV without his instruction, but I knew I didn't need it anymore. I expected him to be displeased with me, but I didn't care. I knew, that I knew, what I knew had happened.

As predicted, he wasn't pleased with me. In fact, I received a scolding. He emphatically explained to me that once someone stops an anti-retroviral drug, the HIV virus mutates itself against the drug, and the chemical in the drug is usually no longer effective. I had no more options for other drugs. I had tried them all, and they were either ineffective or I was allergic to them. He was very agitated with me. He gave me my lab order for blood work and then left the exam room.

Two weeks passed, and I had not heard from my doctor concerning my numbers. The two most important lab results are the T-cell count and the viral load, which as I explained earlier, is a direct count of how much virus is within a drop of blood. I called to get the results, and a nurse came on the phone and informed me my T-cells were 254 (up from 165), which meant that I was out of the "danger zone," and my viral load was 36,000 (down from 187,000). I was moving in the right direction, which had never happened before. It may not sound like much of an improvement, but the real difference was in how I was feeling. Yes, the virus was still there, but it wasn't affecting my health any more. The virus wasn't ravaging my body any longer, and I felt like a new person—so far from where I had been.

As the weeks passed, I continued to improve. I tried to stay confident that it was in God's control, that everything would somehow work out. Dad was supporting me by giving me gas money and providing meals and a roof over my head. I was so grateful he was there for me, filling the gap when I really needed him. That, in and of itself, was overwhelming given our differences in the past.

Soon, out of nowhere, I received a phone call from my attorney. She was hired to facilitate the American's with Disabilities Act complaint I had filed against my employer. Many things facilitated this action; but nonetheless, it was a necessary evil under the circumstance.

She informed me a settlement had been reached, and this legal nightmare would be over soon. It wasn't long before an amicable agreement was reached that would protect both parties in the future. All things were settled very quickly. I was no longer employed.

I knew it was God providing a clear path for my future. There had been so many bad experiences in the past, so many poor choices and horrible mistakes. *How could God love me that much? How could he bless me in such a great way?* I found my confidence in God again. I had no idea what my future held in store for me, but I was confident that God would set me on the right path. After all, God had pulled me out of the deep, dark gapping hole my life had become. He rescued me from a very bleak future and certain death. *What did you save me for? What am I supposed to do with my ransomed life?* The answers to these questions were temporarily illusive, but God soon revealed the answer to at least one of them.

I was soon back on my feet and living on my own again. It felt good. I could feel my life slowly being put back together. I felt the gap closing as my relationships, finances, and faith were being restored. I felt strong enough to start reaching out, making myself vulnerable enough to even think of sharing my life with another person. But this time I started praying that God would send me the right person, someone who would respect me and treat me with dignity and love. Sex didn't matter to me, and I could have cared less about physique or wealth. It didn't matter if he had Aids or some other illness. It was no longer important if he was good looking—all of those things had brought me nothing but pain and despair. God had changed my focus, changed my thinking, but not who I was.

I believe some Christians think that in order to be a "true" Christian, one has to follow and commit to all of their silly rules and expectations, but God took me as I was, loved me as I was, and started working with what I had. I realize that there are many staunch gay haters in this world. It is a true shame many of them hide their prejudice behind Christianity. I could let this detour my intentions of serving God, but this revelation must be shared. The Bible never says anywhere that we have to change for God to love us, only that we totally commit to Him and love Him with all our hearts. And if we believe in Him, we can live without condemnation or fear, *even if we do sin* (John 3:18, Romans 8:1). I know this is a revelation to some because many people believe that they have to try and be perfect so God will love them. Guess what? He already does, and He knows every minute detail of our inner lives. He knows our heart and how we feel. If you're gay, He already knows what you do behind closed doors. He already feels you when you're hurt and left diminished. He already knows those dirty little secrets that you keep hidden from everybody. Surprise!! Yet . . . . HE LOVES YOU ANYWAY!

Jesus' specialty is restoration. He will take the worst offender, the lowest of the low, the most horrible situation and bring that person back to a place of relationship with Him. He will unabashedly take the most defiable situation or circumstance and supernaturally change and control it to work in their favor. He takes away the dark stain in your soul left by the sin in your life and cleans it making you a whole and right person in His sight. It doesn't matter what you've done, how bad you've done it, or the dirtiness of it. Let Him clean it up and, He will, I promise. Better yet, He promises. Look at the story of David for example.

David was, as everybody knows, the boy who slew Goliath. But before that happened, in 1Samuel 16:13 we read that God anointed David with the Spirit of the Lord, and the Lord was with him from that day on. It also says The Lord came upon him in power. After this, the shepherd boy volunteered to go to the front line of the battle against the Philistines. His king blessed him and let him go. David faced a giant of a man named Goliath, and slew him in the name of the Lord (1Samuel 17:45-47). This was the first of many fulfilled promises.

In all of David's future battles, God gave him mercy, favor, or grace (1Samuel 18:14). He consistently won and progressed to lead Judah's army. Now, the king of Judah was Saul, but he was jealous of David because he knew God would one day make him king. In 1Samuel 23:17, Saul tried many times to kill David, but the Lord continually delivered David from the king's wrath. At one point David hid in a cave when he learned that Saul and his army were pursuing him. Saul went into the cave to relieve himself, and David snuck up on him and cut off a piece of Saul's robe without him knowing. But David was convicted by the Lord to spare his master, so David didn't kill him. He called out to Saul and the king turned and realized that David had been in the cave. Then David showed Saul the piece of his garment he had cut off and told Saul he could have killed him if he had wanted to. However, David would not because he did not want evil on his hands and left the vengeance to the Lord.

Later, Saul tries again to kill David, but David prevails. In a later battle with the Philistines, Saul is critically wounded, and he falls on his own sword and takes his own life. The enemy finds his body, and cuts off his head, and hangs his body on the fortress walls to rot.

In the course of time, David is later proclaimed the King of Judah, which was a fraction of Israel. God promises David will rescue Israel from the Philistines again (2Samuel 3:18). David prevails and reunites Israel with Judah under one nation called Israel for which he is anointed as king.

After David settled from his battles, God gave him rest from his enemies. He promises David, *Your house and your kingdom will endure forever before me; your throne will be established forever (2Samuel 7:16).* This promise is fulfilled through Jesus Christ since Jesus comes from the blood line created by David's descendants.

It is obvious God loved and protected David through many circumstances that David encountered. God's grace was sufficient for every situation David came up against and fulfilled every promise made on David's behalf. Do you think God turned from David when he sinned? Is it possible that a sin committed by David, which was so bad that it was punishable by death, would stop God from loving him and blessing him? In Acts 13:22, it says that David was a man after God's own heart. For God searches every heart and understands every motive behind our thoughts (1 Chronicles 28:9). No matter what we do, or when the faults and failures of our human condition prevail, God sees our heart and what our true motivations and intentions happen to be. David's son Solomon prayed

God would deal with each man according to all he does, for God alone knows the hearts of all men (1Kings 8:39).

This was never more evident than when David committed adultery and was responsible for the death of his mistress' husband. In 2Samuel Chapter 11 we discover that David lusted after Bathsheba, slept with her, and they conceived a son together. To make matters even worse, David plotted to have her warrior husband sent to the front lines of the battlefield, hoping he would be killed, as he was. When Bathsheba learned of her husband's death, she mourned. After a time, David sent for her and they were married. David admitted, *"I have sinned against the Lord."* David's lamenting is evident in Psalm 38 (NIV).

O Lord, do not rebuke me in your anger

Or discipline me in your wrath.

For your arrows have pierced me,

And your hand has come down upon me.

Because of your wrath there is no health in my body; my

bones have no soundness because of my sin.

My guilt has overwhelmed me like a burden too heavy to

bear.

But, David was reconciled to God because David's heart was pure toward God. Proverbs10:12 says that Hatred stirs up dissension, but love covers all wrongs. He listened to His voice in that quiet still presence in his soul. Not only that, but David was obedient to God and listened to God's wisdom. We find this perfect example in Psalm 51 where David confesses his sin and asks for God's pardon.

Psalm 51 (NIV)
Have mercy on me,
O God, according to your unfailing love;
According to your great compassion, blot out my
transgressions.
Wash away all my iniquity and cleanse me from sin.
For I know my transgressions, and my sin is always
before me.
Against you, you only, have I sinned and done what
is evil in your sight, so that you are proved right when you
speak and justify when you judge.
Surely you desire truth in the inner parts;
You teach me wisdom in the inmost place.
Create in me a pure heart, O God, and renew a
steadfast spirit within me.
Do not cast me from your presence or take your
Holy Spirit from me.
Then I will teach transgressors your ways, and sinners
will turn back to you.
O Lord, open my lips, and my mouth will declare your praise.
The sacrifices of God are a broken spirit;
A broken and contrite heart,

O God, you will not despise.

God pardoned David, though he still paid for his sin. Sometimes we suffer the consequence of our actions. For we reap what we sow. Galatians 6:7 teaches us God cannot be mocked (or fooled). Do not be deceived. A man reaps what he sows. But He does see our repentant heart. And if your heart is true, God will pardon you, forgive you, and show you mercy and grace. This is the greatest gift God can give us: to save us from what we deserve or earned through our actions. Let the Lord protect you from what *you* deserve.

Chapter 19

Seven Sevens

*In whom we have redemption through His blood,
The forgiveness of sins, according to the riches of
His grace.*

Ephesians 1:7 (KJV)

I must introduce this chapter as my personal testimony.

First, I must thank God for His mercy and grace. If it were not for either of these gifts from God, I would not be writing this testimony. They are so precious and yet immeasurable. God has not only saved me, blessed me, healed me and rescued me, He has continually nurtured and taught me through His word and The Holy Spirit.

I never realized when I was growing up, just what God's personality was like. I just believed He was out there somewhere in the Universe watching what everyone was doing. I had no clue or awareness God was actually participating in our everyday lives. That concept seemed too unfathomable to me. And even though He proved himself many times to me, I still didn't have a relationship" with Him. I progressed to believing that He sometimes intervened or even sometimes performed a miracle, but those graces were reserved for the perfect Christians or "the saints." What is a perfect Christian?

As many people believe, I thought being a Christian meant that you were perfect. Or better yet, if you went to church, you were infallible. Because of the examples around me; friends at church, the pastor, and, in general, all people in church, acted as if they didn't do anything wrong. As I became a young adult in church I began to see people in church weren't perfect. We were all ordinary, imperfect people gathering together on Sunday morning to worship The Lord. We all made our "mistakes" and people were just *trying* to be perfect. Actually, most were just living in their own little bubble and ignoring any of the lessons we were listening to every Sunday, living whatever way they wanted during the week and showing up on Sunday, only to make an impression. It didn't make sense to me at all. I guess my concept of God lacked any personal connection. People were friendly but not engaged with each other. Many times they would be nice to my face and then I would learn that they had made hurtful or derogatory remarks about me when I wasn't around to hear them.

The facts pointed towards understanding that there was an unwritten scale when it came to our mistakes. Sins were judged upon how bad the mistake was when measured on this scale. People who made simple or "forgivable" mistakes were overlooked or judged to the minimum standard when it came to their sin. Others were judged harshly and chastised for their unforgivable "mistake" or shortcoming. Those people were shunned and avoided in the church, causing unnecessary pain to that person, eventually leading to separation from people they trusted. The true fact of the matter is explained in Romans 3:23: *for all have sinned and fall short of the glory of God.* The verse makes no distinction of people, only that all people are sinners. It doesn't matter what social class they are, it doesn't matter how much money they have, and it doesn't even matter how good they are. All of us sin every day. Just read any part of the Old Testament. The examples of common sin are abundant. The only "perfect Christian" was Christ. Christ was all man, but also, all God; therefore, his life, crucifixion, burial and resurrection gives us our right standing with God. God's righteousness is imputed to us through Jesus Christ. There is no possible way we can make ourselves right before God without Christ. There is no chance for us to escape this fundamental truth or shove it in a closet. We all have to face our wrong doings and confess them to God.

In the previous chapter we learned from Psalm 51 in the very first sentence, that David cried out for mercy. But what exactly is mercy? Webster's Dictionary describes it as a compassion or forbearance, especially if that subject is under your power or authority. It is also described as blessing that is an act of divine favor. God is divine. Blessings and favor are from Him. And according to Webster's, it is an act, something God does. It is unmerited or undeserved and is born out of love. It is a compassionate act coming from genuine love. We have all had to give it to others at some point, and we all have received it also.

Romans 12:8 describes mercy as a gift from God we are to share cheerfully because God shares it with us. We would be wise to remember God will not abandon or forsake us because He is merciful, and we are also supposed to ask Him for mercy as David did. James 2:13 says, *Mercy triumphs over judgment.* It is God's trump card over condemnation because He doesn't want us to live under the burden of judgment. Furthermore, it is The Lord's great love that causes His compassion to never fail (Lam.3:22), and it is renewed every single day. It never runs out or is diminished. It may be because we use it up every day. First Peter, verse 3 explains that in His mercy we are given new birth into a living hope through Christ. And that we are also granted an inheritance (eternal life) that can never perish, spoil, or fade, and God shields us by His power until He comes to this earth again. What better promise is there than that?

You might also wonder how God distributes His mercy, or how does He bestow that mercy to us. The answer is found in John 1:16-17, *From the fullness of His (Jesus Christ) grace we have all received one blessing after another. For the law was given through Moses; grace and truth came through Jesus Christ.*

And also from Romans 5:15 states, *How much more did God's grace and the gift that came by the grace of the one man, Jesus Christ, overflow to the many.* So now we understand that mercy comes from God and grace comes through Jesus Christ. We also learn more about grace in Romans chapter 11. Grace is not earned through anything we can do, but it is granted, otherwise, grace wouldn't be grace. It is also a gift, justified through our believing (faith) in Christ. It is bestowed in the blink of an eye the very moment you believe in Jesus and ask Him to come into your heart. All you have to do is ask.

Remember earlier we looked at Romans 3:23 about mercy, now look at the remainder of the thought process in the next scripture, Romans 3:24: *"and are justified, freely by His grace through the redemption that came by Christ Jesus."* Are you getting it? Our only action is to ask for forgiveness, and Christ does the rest. You might think that being a Christian is weak, although it is true that you have to become humble as a child to come to Christ earnestly. Second Corinthians 12:9 explains Christ's grace is sufficient for you, for His power is made perfect in your weakness. In other words, when you become lesser, His grace is sufficient, and His power makes up the difference. Better yet, grace never leaves you. You have absolutely nothing to loose and everything wonderful to gain. Romans 5:20-21 says it perfectly, *But where sin increased, grace increased all the more, so that, just as sin reigned in death, so also grace might reign through righteousness to bring eternal life through Jesus Christ our Lord.* God's perfect salvation.

God's perfect number is seven. His words are purified as silver is purified seven times and made flawless (Psalm 12:6). He rested on the seventh day (the completion of one week) of creation and made it holy (Genesis 2:3). Joseph mourned after his father Jacob for seven days completing the grieving process (Genesis 50:10). The angel Gabriel declared seventy sevens for the atonement of sin so righteousness could be ushered in, referring to Jesus' sacrifice on the cross (Daniel 9:24). Jesus spoke seven times from the cross as His life was made complete (Luke 23:34, 23:43; John 19:26; Mathew 27:46; John 19:28, 30, and Luke 23:46). Offerings and sacred feasts were based on sevens. Sacrifices in the Old Testament were commanded using seven sprinkles of blood (Leviticus 4:6). God drove seven nations out of the land of Canaan before the Israelites entered the promised land (Deuteronomy 7:1). Jesus multiplied seven loaves to feed the multitude (Mathew 15:34-36).

All of these events had one thing in common. It was to make the event perfect according to God—perfect for His blessing and perfect before something else could be accomplished. In my own life there have been many "sevens".

And though not realizing it at the time, but in retrospect, I have been able to see how God worked, even through tragedy, to complete a lesson I needed to learn or bring His blessing.

I will provide a brief synopsis of these events since you have already read the details of most them. And by the way, there are seven of them. (1)From the time I was married to Mona until the divorce was fourteen years. I can only surmise that the marriage lasted for two sevens, as I had not yet come to grip with my truth concerning my homosexuality. (2)Mona and I were married seven years before our first child was born. I fulfilled my duty by providing a son and an heir. My daughter was born in the middle of the next seven. (3)During this same seven years, I started a journey to forgive Jett (see chapter 1), which took seven years of struggling and searching to understand. (4)There was a seven year time period from the divorce to my reconciliation with God. Half of that time was spent in total rebellion to God, which caused seemingly permanent damage to my future. (5)I was gainfully employed by an employer for three sevens or twenty-one years. The first seven was all about learning, the second was about relationships and conflicts with co-workers, and the third was about final enjoyment. Each of these phases was brought to completion without any control by my actions. (6)The sixth seven brought to fruition was actually a time span of twenty-one years also. I will tell you about it in the next chapter, which will bring me up to the near present. (7)The last seven was from the time of my redemption and healing to the present. It has actually been fourteen years, or double the blessing.

In all of these events in my life, there was one thing they all had in common. God was in control. Jeremiah 10:23 shows us that it is not for man to direct his steps but God. He controlled when everything happened, where it took place, who was involved, and how it came to pass. Yes, I was a participant, and yes, I acted selfishly which caused deep hurt in times past, but God ordered my footsteps. I think He did this to protect me, teach me, and show me His love; all of which have brought me to this place of liberty.

The liberty that God has granted to accomplish His goal for my life is explained in Galatians 5:13-14. It says, *You, my brothers, were called to be free. But do not use your freedom to indulge in sinful nature; rather serve one another in love. The entire law is summed up in a single command: Love your neighbor as yourself.* And, because God has directed my footsteps and shown me many things, I have learned God's personality. I know Him as my Father, my Counselor, my Redeemer, my Protector, my Advocate, my Guide and my Savior.

Chapter 20

Victory's Child

*All this is from God,
Who reconciled us to himself through Christ and
gave us the ministry of reconciliation*

2 Corinthians 5:18 (NIV)

Three Years Ago

"Keep your eyes focused on my finger," Derrick said.

I tried, as my therapist repeatedly moved his finger in an ever increasing speed in front of my face. He continued this exploit, as his fingers rapidly waved back and forth.

"Relax", he instructed. After a few moments of this barrage, he asked if I had any visions or pictures appear in my mind.

"No".

He continued for a few more moments and then slowly moved his finger in a circular motion and drew it to his lap. I was motionless. He asked again if I had any pictures flash in my mind.

"No," again.

He then explained that it might take a while for anything to show up, but if it did, I was welcome to contact him at home if I felt I needed to. He professorially stumbled, as he wrote his phone number on a small sheet of paper, and handed it to me before I walked out the door. I had no idea what just happened except to accept his explanation for my plea to help my befuddled mental state.

The procedure performed on me is called EMDR (Eye Movement Desensitization Reprocessing). It is used to bring to present memory any repressed or past memory. It is used by psychiatrists and therapists to get to the root of a problem. It is a form of psychotherapy developed by Francine Shapiro in 1989. The main purpose of this type of therapy is to take a distressing memory from life that is inadequately stored and processed in the brain thus causing mental stress in the current state of the patient. It can be used for Post-Traumatic Stress Disorder, Postpartum Depression, traumatic childhood events, anxiety, and even creativity enhancement.

I didn't know why I had been feeling so stressed and full of anxiety in the previous months, but I knew I needed help to get past it. I couldn't sleep, and I was constantly agitated. I was angry and didn't know why. I had prayed and prayed for an answer to this perplexing problem but could find no relief. I thought perhaps it might have something to do with Jett from many years earlier, but I couldn't be sure. I felt as though God was forcing me to deal with something. Something unfamiliar. I had obviously been through many stressful and anxiety-ridden situations in the past; although, this time it seemed different and deeper somehow.

The next day I went about doing my normal business. I didn't think about it much. It was only three weeks before Christmas, and I had been very busy. I needed to do some repairs on the kitchen plumbing and decided that it had to be done before the holidays, so I reluctantly jumped to the task. I was working on soldering some copper tubing when I suddenly became very agitated. The task was not hard; I had performed this type of repair many times before. But my mind was not working right. I kept having a flash of a picture come through my mind then quickly pass. It continued to appear then vanish. I didn't know what to think of it, only that it made me very upset. I stopped what I was doing and decided to go and take a quick shower for a break. As I undressed, this image appeared in my mind again, only this time it was as plain as looking in a mirror. It persisted and refused to leave my consciousness. I sat on the bed and started to bawl out of control. I cried and cried with no relief. "Stop it!" I demanded. "Stop it! Stop it! Stop it!" I shouted. My entire body was shaking. I fumbled for the phone number that Derric had given me. I dialed the numbers through my tears, not knowing if I dialed it correctly or not. He answered.

"Derric," I asked.

"Yes," he replied.

"This is Jon."

He quickly blurted, "What are you experiencing?"

"I keep seeing this image and it won't go away. It's like a picture, very clear and very disturbing."

"Can you tell me what it is?" he asked.

I started weeping furiously. "I don't know if I can." I replied. There was a long pause.

"This is so hard to admit," I said.

"It's Okay Jon, no matter what. It's just a memory; it can't hurt you," he proclaimed.

There was another long pause.

"I have the picture of a huge penis in front of my face," I blurted, "just inches away."

"When you're seeing this picture, how old do you feel?"

"About three or four," I answered.

"Do you have any other memory with the picture?" he inquired.

"Yes, I, I . . . put it in my mouth," I answered as my crying turned to sobbing.

"Jon, listen to me. I want you to take your Ativan. How much does it take to put you to sleep?" he asked.

"About two milligrams."

"Take two milligram and go to bed. I want to see you tomorrow at 11A.M. Can you do that?"

"Yes. I'll see you then. Bye," I hung up the phone shaking.

I woke calm the next morning, but very concerned. I arrived at my therapist's office on time and he took me right in. I asked him what was I going to do with this information? He asked several more questions to see if I had any other memories come to the surface. I told him I knew it happened at my Grandmother and Grandfather's at a family Christmas gathering in a spare bedroom. I described the room and also what I was wearing. I held my face in my hands and began crying. He sat patiently until I regrouped. The shame I felt was overwhelming. Disgust overtook me as I tried not force any further memories. I felt extreme betrayal, but I didn't know by whom. I informed Derric I knew it was nothing I had experienced as an adult because of the size. It was huge, and only the very tip of it engulfed my mouth. But who? Who would do this? I asked Derric if this could be the reason I was gay. He explained to me that clinically it was difficult for him to make that assumption, but it was possible.

He further explained that there are many clinical studies that suggest that there is a connection to child molestation and homosexuality, but it could take years of psychotherapy to unlock that answer. I asked him why there was a feeling of euphoria with the memory. He said it is quite common for a victim of rape to feel a sense of satisfaction with the event, but it couldn't be relied upon for a conclusive deduction. *"Rape,"* I thought. Then I had an immediate wave of anger overcome me. He then explained that as time passed, I might remember more. *Oh Great!* I sarcastically thought. I don't want to remember more. I asked him what I do now? I had scheduled a Christmas open house for tomorrow and at this point, I really didn't want to see forty to fifty people. He asked if cancellation was an option. I informed him that at this short notice, probably not. He advised me to pick someone I trusted and felt very secure and comfortable with, and sit with them. He said I might not be the perfect host, but only socialize if I was comfortable with it.

The next day came, and I spent most of the day busy with preparations for the party. I thought about it, of course, but the constant activity helped me keep my focus elsewhere. I was nervous and anxious as the time quickly approached for people to begin arriving. I tried my best to be as gracious and engaged as I could muster, but it was truly difficult. My best friend Joyce arrived, and I immediately felt more comfortable. Joyce knew everything from my past and always had an empathetic heart. I sat with her most of the evening, following my therapist's advice. Before I knew it, the gathering was over, and I was actually glad to see a sink full of dishes. I made it through, thank The Lord.

My therapist was right. As time passed, I was able to remember who committed this atrocity. It was an older family friend of my grandparents. He had two sons, of which, one was gay. I wondered if he had subjected them to this violation. I recently learned that this man passed away. I wondered if he ever confessed his sin to the Lord and went to heaven or hell. I guess I'll have to wait to learn the answer to that question.

I spent the next several weeks dealing with the reality of being raped. It's an odd consciousness with many puzzling questions. I came to the realization that this incident, coupled with the fact of Jett's abuse, certainly affected my trust in people. It all made sense now. Looking back, there have been very few places that have given me security. I suppose it is why I moved so many times and always looked for safety—or at least the feeling of security. *Would I always be like this? Will this new information help me overcome my fear of people?* But deeper questions still remained. Why was I afraid of talking in front of people. Why did even small crowds make me anxious? Would I ever feel confident again? Would I ever trust people again?

It was now a week before Christmas, when I received an unexpected phone call. It was Jett. He was calling to RSVP to an invitation I had sent him for an annual Christmas dinner I do for the family every year. Although I hadn't heard from him in twenty-one years, I always sent him invitations to family functions. He asked how I was doing then asked if he could come to the dinner. I told him that he was always welcome, and I would be glad to see him. I gave him directions to my house, and the short conversation ended. I didn't know what to think. Talk about anxiety, Whew! I immediately started to analyze the situation and reconcile this to everything that had happened in the past two weeks. *Why now Lord? What is going on?*

The very next day I received a Christmas card in the mail. I didn't recognize the return address but opened it anyway. It wasn't a card but a Christmas letter. It read as follows:

<u>My Christmas Wish</u>

Every December,
I try to reflect on just one part of the Christmas story.
The people, places and meanings involved in the very
first Christmas story. Doing this has been a blessing to
me and has helped me take to heart the true meaning of
the Season.

This year my thoughts turn to the people that came to
worship and see the Christ child,
the shepherds and wise men.
I can't imagine what it would be like
to see the sky light up,
to see the angels or hear them telling me the good news
of Christmas.
I can't imagine either, studying hard to figure out why
we should follow a star to see a newborn baby.
I am sure they had to wonder "is this really right?"
Oh how wonderful and joyous it must have been,
for both groups, when they realized who the baby was!
I am sure they stood in awe!

The thought that crosses my mind the most is,
how different these two groups were, and yet they ended
up standing in front of the same child, knowing that this
baby would change the world. From the very start Christ
shows us that He came for everyone. The rich, the wise,
and the lowly. The one that has a simple job of watching
sheep,
to someone who has connections to the powerful,
and those that just stand out in a field.

No matter who we are,
we all have a place in front of the Savior.

We all have a place because we all need a God that
saves us from the things in this world.
We all have a place because God loves us all.
When you get a phone call that upsets you or changes
your world,
when sickness comes to you or someone you love,
when addiction pulls your family apart,
when consequences of wrong decisions catch up with
you, when a storm damages your house,
when you lose a job, when grief enters your life;
We all have a place in front of the Savior.

On a warm summer evening, when someone you love
graduates, when you buy a new home, when you start
something new in life, when you get married, when you
see babies born, when you see the autumn color of the
changing leaves, when you see the new Spring come;
We all have a place in front of the Savior

Christ came so that we might have life and that we
might have it more abundantly. God is love and He does
not want to see us hurt, even though we sometimes hurt
in this life. That is just how things are on this earth, but
if we have a place in front of the Savior, we can trust
and know that everything will be all right.

When you see a manger scene this year, I hope you
will think about your place in front of the Savior of the
world. Maybe like wise men, you might wonder "is this
really right?", but they accepted Him and worshipped the
baby boy who would grow up to die on a cross, then rise

from the grave. My wish is that you know, accept, and stand in awe; realizing,
You have a place in front of The Savior!

I fell to my knees and started to weep uncontrollably. I couldn't stop. I hadn't cried that hard since Mom passed away. Even so, Christ was full in my heart and comforting me. Suddenly it all made sense and I no longer wondered "why." I didn't question my illness and ask "why" any longer. I didn't question why Mom was taken so early. I didn't question the rape I had long forgotten. I no longer questioned the reason for Jett's abuse and his absence in my life. I no longer questioned all of the wrong decisions I had made, because I knew that I had a place in front of the Savior, and that He cared so very deeply about what I was feeling in my heart. God showed me He doesn't always answer the "why's", but He does give us peace through the Holy Spirit. He lifted the anxiety and calmed my spirit. It no longer mattered why Jett was coming to my house after all this time; I was just glad he was.

Since that time, I have often remembered that prose that arrived so unexpectedly in my mailbox. I have often remembered the presence of abuse in my life. I have often pondered my illness . . . but all with understanding and peace. I'll know the reason someday when I arrive in heaven, and until then, I'm letting Christ heal me and comfort me. I know it doesn't matter to Him that I'm gay, only that I behave Christ-like. I know He sees the people and my hurt when they reject or make fun of me, and as I seek Him, he heals my wounds. I have profound assurance that I will go to heaven when I die, and Christ comforts me in those thoughts of death. I know He protects and guides the footsteps of my children because I pray for them every single day, and I know God hears me and honors that request. I know someday I will find a church that allows me to be who I am in Christ, no matter what my background. I know God will continue to check and balance me with His love and compassion because I am one of His children. Are You? Do you have this confidence that Jesus can stand in the gap? Remember, *You* have a place in front of the Savior.

Bibliography

The Holy Bible, Old and New Testaments
King James Version (KJV)
Royal Publishers, Nashville, TN
Copyright 1971

The Holy Bible, Old and New Testaments
New International Version (NIV)
Rainbow Studies, Inc. El Reno, OK
Copyright 1996

Strong, James. Strong's Exhaustive Concordance of the Bible
Abingdon Press
Copyright 1890

Webster's Ninth New Collegiate Dictionary
Miriam-Webster, Inc. Springfield, Massachusetts.
Copyright 1991